Newstweek

Fixing the facts.

CW01080709

Sniff, Scrape, Crawl...
{on privacy, surveillance and our shadowy data-double}

– Renée Turner

<u>Today, the border between the public and private is porous</u>. Unlike the ominous spectre of surveillance depicted in George Orwell's Nineteen Eighty-Four, current methods of information gathering are much more subtle, 'friendly', and woven into the fabric of our everyday lives. Customer cards give instant access to discounts, while shopping habits are simultaneously registered. Through behavioural tracking, Amazon tells us which books we might like, Google uniquely tailors its advertising and search results, and Last.fm connects us to people with similar music tastes.

Immersed in social media, we commit to binding contracts and agree to 'terms of use' that would baffle a lawyer, if anyone actually bothered to read the legalese. Nonetheless, having sealed the blind deal with a click, we Twitter our subjectivities in less than 140 characters, contact our long lost friends on Facebook, and mobile-upload our geotagged videos on YouTube. Where once surveillance technologies were associated with the agencies of the government and the military, the web has fostered a participatory and less optically driven means of both monitoring and monetizing our intimately lived experiences. And all of this invisible yet pervasive surveillance is seductively packaged in the language of sociability. Capitalising on our gregarious nature, we are encouraged to share it, like it, tweet it and retweet it. After all, it's about us – who we are, what we want and most importantly, how they can best profit from delivering their coveted commodities and services to us.

A silent listener to our streaming confessions, the ambient social network envelops itself around our rituals, banalities and routines and traces the specificities of our dataset, or rather our shadowy data-double. Crawling and scraping, it creates a portrait of not only who we are as individuals, but also our demographic character, status and potential future self. Just as our data-double grows exponentially through these infinite feedback loops, the debate on privacy also proliferates. While discussions on the value of public space and the commons have regrettably waned, privacy has become the zone of contention for lawyers, large corporations, governments and individuals, who all have much at stake.

Sniff, Scrape, Crawl.... is the result of trying to make sense of these debates. It began as collaborative research between the Master Media

Design and Communication course at the Piet Zwart Institute and Creating 010 Hogeschool Rotterdam. In the Fall of 2011, the Institute hosted a series of workshops, lectures and screenings. As a follow-up, students, staff and guest lecturers presented their results in the form of two panels at ISEA, Istanbul 2011. This book consolidates these research efforts. Bringing together artists, programmers, theorists, students and staff, contributions vary in tone and approach, and critically responds, at times even irreverently, to our idiosyncratic relation to privacy.

In My Meta Is Your Data, Nicolas Malevé interrogates contexts of interpretation to illustrate their importance. Beginning with the rapid consolidation of the web under a few large corporations, Malevé explains how systemic ambiguity is exploited to coerce users into submitting more data. He questions how social platforms are integrated into activist practices, and points to potential problems if corporate fidelity is swayed. Finally, he maps the perfect storm, where Web 2.0 network topologies and economies come together with Internet Service Providers to potentially monitor and control user access to data. Rather than ending apocalyptically, Malevé points to projects like OpenStreetMap as another possible model, which harnesses its own context of interpretation through an alternative working methodology and mode of user governance.

The Discrete Dialogue Network is a project that also represents an alternative to online social networks. Working with simple stickers, mobile phones and a voice messaging system, the project operates like a Situationist psychogeographical dérive, where voice, story and place are intimately woven together. Unlike a conventional online network, nothing is tracked or monitored. Instead, The Discrete Dialogue Network relies on chance encounters and the specificities of a particular place to evoke personal associations. Spread across the city by individual anonymous users, messages are left like traces of graffiti that form loosely knit connections tying geography and narrative across an urban landscape.

Of course the distinction between the online and physical world has never been strictly divided. The ambient social network absorbs us, physical spaces collapse into the digital, and the other way around. In Future Guides for Cities, Michelle Teran highlights precisely this seamless flow between registers. Online maps and self-generated media are archival material for her explorations of the tension between public and private space. Tracking a single user's YouTube uploads, she oscillates between voyeur and stalker. While navigating across her computer screen to eventually arriving physically at her destination, she reflects on the history of domestic space, fears of home invasion, the homogenising forces shaping today's public life, and the possibilities of encountering the stranger in the city.

Just as algorithms might create an opportunity for meeting strangers, the question arises of how they might shape and influence our destiny. Amy Suo Wu's contribution is a somewhat playful, speculative and dystopic depiction of precisely this scenario. A short piece of fiction, Benji ™ is the imagined biography of the child of Sergey Brin, the co-founder of Google, and his wife, Anne Wojcicki, the co-founder of 23andme.com, a genomics and biotechnology company. Pitched somewhere between the rhetoric of entrepreneurialism, new age mysticism and biotech hype, Benji is larger than life, a self-made man and the inventor of a business empire. Matching careful DNA analysis with online advertising, Benji serves up the ultimate in 'search', where rendered results are not only the perfect mirror of the self, but also a prediction of the self yet to come. In this eerie dream-like scenario, market indicators are transformed into modern soothsayers in whom all trust can be placed.

But what if users don't want to become one with their data double, and would rather disconnect their individual profile from their specific dataset? Anonymity has become the exalted answer to the dilemma. From 4chan's foster child, Anonymous, to the practice of IP address cloaking, to those who would rather dwell in the shelter of the darknet, the desire to remain unidentified appears strong. Moving beyond the hype, in The Spectre of Anonymity, Seda Gürses looks at the historical uses of anonymity through traditional folksongs and their relation to authorship and the collective. She questions how these dynamics function online in connection to an individual's dataset. Finally, analysing anonymity as both a technical and strategic device, she elaborates on its strengths and vulnerabilities in order to show there is no one-size-fits-all approach.

Taking a completely different direction, Inge Hoonte's Dear Philip E. Agre, are confessional in tone and reflect on the digital traces of Agre, his writings and the fragile link between people. Having disappeared somewhere between 2008 and 2009, mass appeals were circulated across the web. Finally in 2010 Agre was found, but at his request his whereabouts remain undisclosed. Nevertheless, his essays linger online, and despite not having published in years, his work remains seminal within the research and discourse on digital privacy. Touching on his various writings, Hoonte digresses into anecdote and personal stories to speak about the subtle connections between people, places and random encounters. In her correspondence, the network appears everywhere. Referencing Agre's essay, Welcome to the Always-on World, Hoonte acknowledges: "It's becoming harder and harder to turn off, to be offline, and to be truly alone." The letters are like messages in a bottle set adrift; ultimately they reveal more about the author than the imagined recipient.

This open-ended desire to connect is exactly what the social network exploits and folds back into an infinite set of feedback loops to produce the information economy. Steve Rushton's essay delves further into this system, which perversely thrives on the activity of its users as self-performing subjects. Working across a broad range of examples from reality television to social networks, Rushton wonders what this state of perpetual presentation and performing is doing, meaning how it fuels the mechanisms of commerce and shapes our consciousness. Starting with media activist critique from the sixties and seventies generated by Radical Software, Ant Farm and others, he explains how the a gap has closed between the producer, consumer and spectacle. Instead, we are living in a world where the commodity and the performer are one.

Related to the self-performing subject, in her essay Birgit Bachler speaks of participatory surveillance. As we perform or participate online, we not only watch others, and ourselves but invisible algorithms track the relation between all of these activities. Looking at the interface of Facebook, Bachler shows how we are forced into a set of reductive binary choices. Her deconstruction of the interface is reminiscent of Matthew Fuller's analysis of software and how it habituates and disciplines us.[1] For Bachler the main concern is not only the hidden cost of participatory surveillance, but also how the simple 'user friendly' blue interface may actually be standardising our communication amongst friends.

In a time of participatory surveillance, understanding what is being tracked is one of the most difficult challenges for any user. Clean interfaces and 'one click' settings conceal the way data is gathered and interrelated. However, Naked on Pluto, a multi-player game integrating Facebook, reveals those invisible connections in a playful way. Operating within Facebook's guidelines, the project only uses data that is made accessible when adding any app. But the surprise is one of recontextualisation. As scholars such as Daniel J. Solove and Helen Nissenbaum have argued, integral to our understanding of privacy is the notion of context. [2] If there is a shift of context, and data is moved from one place to another, in this case from Facebook to Pluto, a sense of sudden exposure ensues.

In the end, networks are always vulnerable and ripe for double espionage. That's what projects like Newstweek, Men in Grey, or even loose collectives like Anonymous do. They exploit, distort, propagate and make us aware of the fragility of a system, which on the one hand appears technologically stealth, but on the other, is hung together with criss-crossing cables, hardware and out-dated encryption. They expose the soft penetrable membrane between big media and little gadgets, Internet Service Providers and unprotected wireless networks in homes and Internet cafés. Whether complex or ad hoc, there are always loopholes to be found.

In the age of social networking, privacy is tenuous and elastic. The question is whether we should submit, resist, disconnect, or sabotage in response. Of course to reject the binary, which is crucial to understanding the fluidity of privacy, requires engaging most likely in all of the above. Sniff, Scrape, Crawl... is not only about the mechanisms of surveillance we are subjected to, but it also refers to our own balancing act performed daily within the network, a place where the double bind is perpetually the norm.

[1] For further reading see: **Behind the Blip: essays on the culture of software,** Autonomedia: New York (2003)

[2] For further reading see: **Understanding Privacy,** Daniel J. Solove, Harvard University Press: Cambridge (May 2008) and **Privacy in Context: Technology, Policy, and the Integrity of Social Life,** Helen Nissenbaum, Stanford Law Books: Palo Alto, CA (2009)

My meta is
your data – Nicolas Malevé

"Since the future development of the digital economy depends on large investments, how long can we rely on competition policies to defend net neutrality?"

My meta is
your data – Nicolas Malevé

This text came from my experiences with Constant, [1] a Belgian-based cultural association working with various media since 1997. For the past decade, we have been exploring the potential of the culture of sharing, particularly in the context of artistic, creative and cultural content. In early 2000, we became interested in the way online services provided an infrastructure for sharing and collective production. Later branded as Web 2.0, these services helped popularise Creative Commons licenses. A striking example of this attitude was articulated in the early 'terms of use' of Flickr, a photo sharing service created in 2004 by the startup Ludicorp. It stated: "We encourage users to contribute their creations to the public domain or consider licensing their creations under less draconian terms than have become standards in most jurisdictions [...] Ludicorp undertakes to obey all relevant copyright laws however misguided we may all judge them to be."
Though this initial statement sounded promising, within a few years the rhetoric had completely changed. Big players bought up small platforms in order to expand their services and increase the value of their portfolios. Google bought Blogger and YouTube; Yahoo bought Flickr. Since 2005, the tone has changed dramatically. Now, upon accessing Flickr's copyright policy, we find the standard Yahoo copyright terms. The once-critical perspective has long since been replaced by copyright policies focused on avoiding infringements. Rather than encouraging re-use, policies are now aimed at protection, restriction and enforcement. This shift, and its consequences, should not be underestimated. This is the basis of my reflection on contexts of interpretation and why they matter.

THE ONCE-CRITICAL PERSPECTIVE HAS LONG SINCE BEEN REPLACED BY COPYRIGHT POLICIES FOCUSED ON AVOIDING INFRINGEMENTS.

User data and contexts of interpretation:

On first sight, most services seem to have kept their identity. Browsing Blogger, YouTube and Flickr, each feels like a distinct entity. But the company owning the platform actually controls the policies, and monitors data traffic across the variety of platforms they own. Through this access to user data, the companies learn from user habits, tastes, connections and relationships, and use this knowledge to provide marketing specialists and advertisers with precise statistics and personal profile data. In essence, the function of the Web 2.0 platforms is to transform the mess of social relationships into formalised and comprehensible behaviours. As relational data is of strategic importance for creating valuable user profiles, every single action expressing these connections must be captured. Therefore, the platforms constantly require that you state your preferences and affinities. They constantly provide you with formats, interfaces, and icons with which to express social connections. It is not enough to drop a note or a comment, you have to 'login to like this image,' 'accept a friend request,' or confirm which people you wish to disclose your content to.

THIS PARASITIC FORMALISM OCCURS AT EVERY MOMENT OF DIGITAL SOCIALISATION AND CREATES A CONSTANT FEELING OF AWKWARDNESS.

This parasitic formalism occurs at every moment of digital socialisation and creates a constant feeling of awkwardness: friends on Facebook may only be acquaintances, but the interface forces you to either categorise them as friends, or else refuse to engage with them at all. To promote a 'Tsunami' article, we must click the 'like' button, though everyone understands that 'like' is not a term we would normally be using here. Or consider the peculiarity of being asked to identify familiar people in a picture in order to log in to our account. All these awkward requests can be understood as symptoms of the fact that the context of interpretation is outside of our reach. We are asked to express our likes and dislikes in such a fashion, only because the system requires this kind of structure in order to process the information. How it actually works, we don't know; what we do know is that when we surrender to its ambiguity, the system rewards us. When somebody accepts us as a 'friend', we can access his or her content. Identifying a half-drunk classmate in a blurred photograph allows us to log in to our account. But, as Andrew Goffey and Matthew Fuller explained in their lecture "From Grey Eminence to Grey Immanence: The Ambiguities of Evil Media.": "Crucially, systemic ambiguity is as much about the production as it is about the deciphering of signs. Becoming able to read the shifting balance and distribution of forces in fluctuating patterns of uncertain signs is one thing. Being able to produce such signs, to turn them to your advantage, is another."[2] Web 2.0 capitalises on this systemic ambiguity.

Every single mouse click connecting A to B is thus captured, logged and processed. Since this information is crucial, it needs constant verification – it needs the user's cooperation and care. As a user of social platform and Web 2.0 services, you are put to work. Not only do you produce content and connections, you also have to control the quality of the circulating data. You rate, recommend and report. And the interface rates you back: your performances are public. One can see how many comments and 'likes' you have received, how many people have played your video. You have five hundred 'friends,' five 'badges,' and three 'followers' while you yourself 'follow' one hundred people, and "you haven't added any tip near Vigo, yet."

For their online presence, many activist collectives, though critical of commercial media, use a combination of open-source software and social network add-ons. They are often ambivalent about what to keep under their own control, and what to delegate to online services. Many forms of delegation exist: "follow us on Twitter," "like" this article, "contact us at ..@ gmail.com". As reputation systems are extremely difficult to (re) produce without massive investments, these collectives 'outsource' such systems to social networks. The same is true for any functionalities requiring real-time management of communication with a large user base, connections with cell phones, or specialised features such as maps or videos. The online presence of such groups can be pictured as a thin layer managed by the group itself, superimposed on data from external services: connecting systems, but without any control of how the data is managed and interpreted.

During the student demonstrations that took place in England in 2011, the British police used a technique called kettling. Kettling, as Wikipedia defines it, is "a police tactic for the management of large crowds during demonstrations or protests. It involves the formation of large cordons of police officers who then move to contain a crowd within a limited area. Protesters are left only one choice of exit, determined by the police, or are completely prevented from leaving. In some cases protesters are reported to have been denied access to food, water and toilet facilities for a long period."[3]

SINCE MANY PEOPLE RELY ON THE AUTHENTICITY OF THIS INFORMATION, IDENTIFICATION OF SOURCES IS CRUCIAL.

A group of students and volunteers teamed up to create Sukey, an application informing protesters of the movements of the police, and directions protesters should take in order to avoid being trapped in a cordon.[4] The information is transferred in real time via a web platform to and from mobile phones, and is provided by protesters, observers and people monitoring the news. Since many people rely on the authenticity of this information, identification of sources is crucial.

Sukey searches for messages on Facebook, Twitter, Tumblr and other social networks using the hashtag #Sukey. The results are then filtered using what one of the programmers calls "a kind of algorithmic reputation management."[5] The use of Sukey has proved very useful for protesters who successfully used it to escape kettling. But it has also raised many questions regarding the way it relies on external platforms to establish the reliability and trustworthiness of its sources, in a context where trust is essential. It tapped into the social networks' power to aggregate and spread information and map out relationships, and used this power to distribute strategic information to protesters. But in doing so, it also fed the data-hungry machines of social networks with sensitive information about protesters and their circles of friends.

Using the Web 2.0 to outsource the real-time management of information and the quantification of trust, means relying on parties that have no interest in protecting user information from prying eyes, and are not committed to systematic encryption or erasing logs, but instead run systems designed to eavesdrop and record every possible element of relationality. Past experience has shown how their loyalty, more than often than not, lies with the powers that be.[6] How long before the street corralling gives place to the digital cordon? The example of Sukey is important on more than one level. It questions how activist applications relying on connections to social networks can preserve their autonomy and control the flow of data. It also emphasises the importance of legislation regulating how and when authorities may access information gathered by Web 2.0 platforms.

BUT IN DOING SO, IT ALSO FED THE DATA-HUNGRY MACHINES OF SOCIAL NETWORKS WITH SENSITIVE INFORMATION ABOUT PROTESTERS AND THEIR CIRCLES OF FRIENDS.

Let us now move on, from the general context of social media to the subject of the harmonisation of legal frameworks which regulate the way these media (and their corporate governance) operate within European law. I will attempt to demonstrate how a combination of governmental policies and Web 2.0 data profit schemes could radically transform the Internet as we know it.

Parallel to the development of the Web 2.0, an impressive number of international agreements, directives, legislative bills and draft recommendations have landed on the desks of decision-makers in the USA and Europe (at both EU and national levels). The legal framework regulating the relationship between authorities and user data is currently undergoing a process of harmonisation. Brandishing the spectre of piracy, these agreements invariably emphasise the same point: strengthening cooperation between service providers and the authorities. The negotiators of the Anti-Counterfeiting Trade Agreement wish to promote what they euphemistically refer to as a "cooperation between service providers and right holders to address relevant infringements in the digital environment."[7] The experts consulted by the European Commission provide a more concrete explanation of this cooperation. They consider the service providers in a favourable position to not only "contribute to prevent" but also "terminate" infringements,[8] and therefore suggest to the Commission to "involve them [the service providers] more closely."[9] The Trans-Pacific Trade Agreement proposes that its signatories create "legal incentives" to ensure service providers' cooperation. [10] Clearly, adjusting legal texts in order to promote cooperation between governments and service providers is a recurring theme, meaning service providers are expected to disclose user data to authorities, to assist in monitoring user behaviour, and even to proactively take appropriate punitive actions.

USING THE WEB 2.0 TO OUTSOURCE THE REAL-TIME MANAGEMENT OF INFORMATION AND THE QUANTIFICATION OF TRUST, MEANS RELYING ON PARTIES THAT HAVE NO INTEREST IN PROTECTING USER INFORMATION FROM PRYING EYES, AND ARE NOT COMMITTED TO SYSTEMATIC ENCRYPTION OR ERASING LOGS, BUT INSTEAD RUN SYSTEMS DESIGNED TO EAVESDROP AND RECORD EVERY POSSIBLE ELEMENT OF RELATIONALITY.

But who exactly are these 'service providers'? The definition of the term varies from one text to another. Service providers can either be companies providing access to the Internet (also known as access providers) or companies providing services on the Internet. This rather broad definition can be explained in a historical perspective. Access providers and service providers both followed the same evolutionary path: an assortment of small startup companies, most of which were later bought up by larger ones. As Kleiner and Wyrick strikingly formulate it in their essay "InfoEnclosure 2.0": "The mission of Internet Investment Boom 1.0 was to destroy the independent service provider and put large, well financed, corporations back in the driving seat. The mission of Web 2.0 is to destroy the P2P aspect of the Internet. To make you, your computer, and your Internet connection dependent on connecting to a centralized service that controls your ability to communicate."[111] By reducing the number of access providers and online services to a few big players, a powerful movement of concentration and homogenisation is taking place. The access providers determine how one can access digital communication; the online services increasingly define the framework in which content, contacts and dialogue take place. For governments, gaining access to these central reservoirs of information about their citizens' behaviour becomes a strategic issue. And both access providers and service providers can provide the same 'service': making available their concentrated silos of data.

Currently, although service providers are regularly mentioned, access providers still remain the preferred candidate for this kind of cooperation, as they have complete access to data traffic. But recording, analysing and filtering data traffic costs money. Because governments don't have the money to finance such an infrastructure a new scenario is beginning to take shape, with more clearly defined roles for all parties involved.

THE ACCESS PROVIDERS DETERMINE HOW ONE CAN ACCESS DIGITAL COMMUNICATION; THE ONLINE SERVICES INCREASINGLY DEFINE THE FRAMEWORK IN WHICH CONTENT, CONTACTS AND DIALOGUE TAKE PLACE.

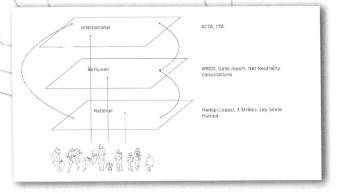

International   ACTA, FTA

European   IPRED, Gallo report, Net Neutrality consultations

National   Hadopi,Loppsi, 3 Strikes, Ley Sinde Humed

Service providers monitor and filter user traffic and cooperate intensively and pre-emptively in the struggle against copyright infringers and criminals, going above and beyond their traditional role of neutral intermediaries. This requires setting up a costly infrastructure, which can then be used by the service providers to allow different levels of access according to the nature of the content being transferred. Because the service providers have concentrated users' attention and interaction into a small number of specific channels, the providers can strike deals with the services: users downloading mp3s from the iTunes Store enjoy full bandwidth, users downloading the same mp3s from Jamendo are allowed only downgraded access. The infrastructure built for surveillance can thus be recycled in order to develop a commercial model of bandwidth discrimination, abandoning the tradition of net neutrality.

THE INFRASTRUCTURE BUILT FOR SURVEILLANCE CAN THUS BE RECYCLED IN ORDER TO DEVELOP A COMMERCIAL MODEL OF BANDWIDTH DISCRIMINATION, ABANDONING THE TRADITION OF NET NEUTRALITY.

Although some elements of this scenario are currently being tested in France, the United Kingdom and the United States, it still clashes with existing competition policies. Recently, Neelie Kroes, European Commission Vice-President for the Digital Agenda, voiced some very strong rhetoric against such traffic discrimination: "Mark my words: if measures to enhance competition are not enough to bring Internet providers to offer real consumer choice, I am ready to prohibit the blocking of lawful services or applications. It's not OK for Skype and other such services to be throttled. That is anti-competitive. It's not OK to rip off consumers on connection speeds." [12] But as she herself needs the cooperation of access providers to finance broadband access (around €200 billion) for European citizens, will she be able to refuse them such a return on their investment? [13] Since the future development of the digital economy depends on large investments, how long can we rely on competition policies to defend net neutrality?

To summarize: I have shown how the commercial scheme of Web 2.0 was built on the exploitation of user data, and how a collusion of interests between access providers and service providers could bring about a discrimination of access. The concentration of user information in Web 2.0 databases, and the monitoring of traffic by access providers, creates an enormous reservoir of data on citizens' behaviour. Collection of user data is defined by the terms of use of web platforms, and government access to the information collected is defined by legal frameworks and international agreements which are constantly being developed and refined. The legislation currently under way, and the social networks' terms of use, both demonstrate a similar attitude toward the gathering of user data: they disregard the users' ability to discuss, interpret and change this data. In these contexts, user data is not seen an area for cooperation, and the context in which it is interpreted is deliberately kept out of the users' reach. Furthermore, the very process by which this data is stored and modified remains opaque as well as unilateral. At this point, we should consider the Open-StreetMap (OSM) project, which deals more intelligently with user data, and provides a wonderful example of how terms of use and legal decisions can be taken collectively by users; how a context of interpretation can be designed and maintained by a community.

IN THESE CONTEXTS, USER DATA IS NOT SEEN AN AREA FOR COOPERATION, AND THE CONTEXT IN WHICH IT IS INTERPRETED IS DELIBERATELY KEPT OUT OF THE USERS' REACH.

In short, OSM is a Wikipedia for maps. Users upload geolocated information (GPS traces) to a server; they can then edit, clean up and enhance this information, before it is used to produce online maps. The site's database can be downloaded to create 'mirror' sites or geolocative services, or any other project requiring geodata. At various levels, the OSM project shows a clearly different approach compared to Web 2.0 data practices. Whereas Web 2.0 services provide users with an interface that conceals metadata and logged behaviour, OSM is proactively 'open' about its use of user data. The OSM experience starts by learning to think differently about the GPS device. Rather than merely follow its instructions, apprentice cartographers are asked to focus on how the device graphically renders their GPS trace and logs their itineraries. These logs can be uploaded to the project's database, and further processed to indicate roads, buildings, rivers, etc. Whereas recent legal developments in this area been controversial and non-transparent, in OSM the user community establishes its own rules through discussion and consensus.

An important legal question recently arose, which provided an excellent insight into the dynamics of this user community. A few years after OSM was launched, participants realised that the license under which they were distributing the data included in the maps was not legally valid: geographical data does not fall under the scope of free licenses which protect 'original' creations such as literary works. 'Objective' information, such as geographical coordinates, falls into another legal category in most legislation. The OSM foundation, which facilitates the operation of the project, set up a process of consultation (lasting several months) with participants including legal specialists who volunteered their services. The goal was to redefine the terms of use in such a way that everyone can simply use the OSM data, but that users are required to add to the OSM database any corrections, additions or other modifications they make to the data. It was interesting to observe how participants convinced each other, in online and offline discussions, of the importance of protecting the open-source nature of the software, and preventing their common effort from being distorted while still keeping it open; and how they accepted to formalise their participation somewhat, in other to safeguard the fundamental motives behind their participation. This type of discussion demonstrates once again how anything considered as 'public' is subject to a constant process of re-negotiation.

IT WAS INTERESTING TO OBSERVE HOW PARTICIPANTS CONVINCED EACH OTHER, IN ONLINE AND OFFLINE DISCUSSIONS, OF THE IMPORTANCE OF PROTECTING THE OPEN-SOURCE NATURE OF THE SOFTWARE.

sniff scrape crawl

What these examples show, is that there is no inevitable fate
forcing us to accept that the context of interpretation of the
data we produce using digital technologies should be kept out
of our reach. The OSM project demonstrates that social dynamics and dialogue can produce comprehensive agreements
on how to collectively share data, and how to take the necessary legal decisions collectively. It shows the power of open
platforms and the difference we can make by being actively
engaged in creating and maintaining a context of interpretation.

OSM is, although remarkable, by no means an isolated project
in terms of its philosophy and development. Today we need
strategies for making collective practices of data care a part of
the legal dialogue. But more than ever, we need to experiment
with collective forms of management, in which the administra-
tion of user data is not synonymous with policing or profiling.
We can begin with simple steps, such as running a group's blog
or imagining new scenarios for exchanging data, before moving on to more complex undertakings such as installing a web
server, exploring new platforms and different policies, taking
part in their design, promoting them, and participating in their
maintenance. The task is huge, but it can be broken down into
smaller individual actions. What we will gain in freedom and
knowledge, we will have to pay for with time and/or money.
But if we wish to gain access to the contexts of interpretation,
free is better than 'free'.

[1] **Constant**, http://www.constantvzw.org
(accessed June 06, 2011)

[2] Matthew Fuller & Andrew Goffey, **"From Grey Eminence
to Grey Immanence: The Ambiguities of Evil Media"**, a
video recording of the conference, November 28, 2009
http://video.constantvzw.org/vj12/Goffey-Fuller.ogv
(accessed June 06, 2011)

[3] Kettling, http://en.wikipedia.org/wiki/Kettling
(accessed June 06, 2011)

[4] The official homepage of Sukey, http://www.sukey.org
(accessed June 06, 2011).

22

[5] Tannara Yelland, **"British students create program to warn protesters about police movement"**, February 11, 2011 http://tannarayelland.wordpress.com/2011/02/11/british-students-create-program-to-warn-protesters-about-police-movement/ (accessed June 06, 2011)

[6] Napakatbra, **"Yahoo balance votre vie privée pour 60 dollars,"** December 10, 2009 http://www.lesmotsontunsens.com/yahoo-balance-votre-vie-privee-pour-60-6438 (accessed June 06, 2011)

[7] **Anti-Counterfeiting Trade Agreement,** English Version, page 2, November 2010 http://trade.ec.europa.eu/doclib/html/147937.htm (accessed June 06, 2011)

[8] "REPORT FROM THE COMMISSION TO THE EUROPEAN PARLIAMENT, THE COUNCIL, THE EUROPEAN ECONOMIC AND SOCIAL COMMITTEE AND THE COMMITTEE OF THE REGIONS, Application of Directive 2004/48/EC of the European Parliament and the Council of 29 April 2004 on the enforcement of intellectual property rights" December 12, 2010 http://eur-lex.europa.eu/LexUriServ/LexUriServ.do?uri=COM:2010:0779:FIN:EN:HTML (accessed June 06, 2011)

[9] Ibid.

[10] **"The complete Feb 10, 2011 text of the US proposal for the TPP IPR chapter",** Leaked source published by Knowledge Ecology International, March 10, 2011 http://www.keionline.org/node/1091 (accessed June 06, 2011)

[11] Dmytri Kleiner & Brian Wyrick, **"InfoEnclosure 2.0"**, January 26, 2007, http://www.metamute.org/en/InfoEnclosure-2.0 (accessed June 06, 2011)

[12] Neelie Kroes, **"The internet belongs to all of us"** Press conference on Net Neutrality Communication Brussels, April 19, 2011 "http://europa.eu/rapid/pressReleasesAction.do?reference=SPEECH/11/285&format=HTML&aged=0&language=EN&guiLanguage=en (accessed June 06, 2011)

[13] Neelie Kroes, **"A big week for broadband"**, September 23, 2010, http://blogs.ec.europa.eu/neelie-kroes/a-big-week-for-broadband/ (accessed June 06, 2011)

I would like to thank the people who helped me to clarify my thoughts and turn my initial draft into proper English: Renée Turner, Joe Monk and Steve Rushton. Without the impressive research of Michel Cleempoel (and his friendship), I would not have been able to write a single line. This text is an echo of an ongoing conversation with Seda Gürses, the members of Constant, Rafaella Houlstan-Hasaerts and, last but not least, Laurence Rassel.

sniff scrape crawl

Discrete Dialogue Network

ID #
_____

CALL

The Discrete Dialogue
Network is a telephony-
based communication system
designed for leaving
anonymous voice messages
to strangers in public
space. Conceived as an
alternative to the flatness
of other social networks,
it is a medium operating
outside the business of
profile pictures, status
updates and "Like"-
buttons.

25

Unheard poetry in a
backyard, the secrets of
an abandoned lot, gossip
in the ladies room and
wisdom from a park bench,
now all can be shared
with people you may not
even want to know
or even add to your
LinkedIn network.

PHOTO TAKEN BY:NATAŠA SIENČNIK

The Discrete Dialogue
Network embraces exchange
with people outside
of your friend lists,
capitalizes on the
significance of place,
and draws invisible
connections between
strangers as they leave
messages at the same
location.

The only way to access
the network is to find a
sticker-tag that has been
left behind by someone.
Each has a unique number
that serves as the link
between a specific location
and voicemail box. When
calling, a person can
hear all previously left
messages and record their
own messages for others to
listen to.

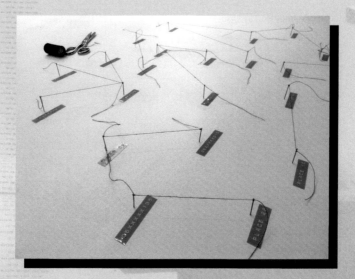

The Discrete Dialogue
Network does not require
registration or ask for
personal data. Since it
is based on the Open
Source telephony software
freeswitch, enthusiasts
are encouraged to build
their own network through
an online toolkit.

http://
discretedialoguenetwork.
org/

Future Guides
for Cities – Michelle Teran

"I sit in front of a computer screen and observe the physical construction of a house. From an apartment in Berlin, I watch a collection of twenty-four YouTube videos of an event taking place in a different city, in another part of the country."

Future Guides
for Cities – Michelle Teran

Above the earth, I am scanning. I travel a landscape of images, formed by the occupants of a city of e-maps created by amateurs. I have a bird's eye view of a neighbourhood and search for moments of video wedged into the terrain, video fragments that tell me where to go. Weightlessness leads to orientation. I am looking for something, I am looking for someone to meet.

I begin this essay with a personal experience, observing a private moment now made public. The focus of this text is to examine private narratives in public spaces, and the relationships between information and the city. This text, and my personal experience, both explore the spatial and social constructions of the relationships between private and public, the notions of stranger and strangeness, and how social and spatial homogeneity are constructed and mediated through the potential social impacts of disclosing information online. The critical locus of this project is the result of my role as an artist working with media and performance during the past decade, creating site-specific performances and urban interventions that explore the relationships that occur during the self-production of media and city.

THE CRITICAL LOCUS OF THIS PROJECT IS THE RESULT OF MY ROLE AS AN ARTIST WORKING WITH MEDIA AND PERFORMANCE DURING THE PAST DECADE, CREATING SITE-SPECIFIC PERFORMANCES AND URBAN INTERVENTIONS THAT EXPLORE THE RELATIONSHIPS THAT OCCUR DURING THE SELF-PRODUCTION OF MEDIA AND CITY.

I sit in front of a computer screen and observe the physical construction of a house. From an apartment in Berlin, I watch a collection of twenty-four YouTube videos of an event taking place in a different city, in another part of the country. A woman and a man, Antje and Carsten, begin to build a life together. The creation of a home, and what eventually takes place inside it, is dutifully recorded on camera and put online for a global audience. The videos are superimposed on a satellite image of the city, which is how I have found the videos and can now watch them. Over the course of a year, a house emerges from a vacant lot on the edge of the city, and is eventually painted and then furnished. Parties take place there. Friends are invited inside. I observe the social construction of a home. I am in the home, and they invite me inside by making and posting these videos. It is a publication of privacy; a state of being private in a public, digital space. As I watch the house being constructed, I wonder where the house is, and what it would be like to live there. I wonder how it would feel to be invited into this space, what it would be like to meet them.

I am now in the house.

VIDEO TITLE: Construction of C&A's house is rapidly progressing. Work is being done on the heating, plumbing, walls and electricity.[1]

He walks, breathlessly. The walls are built but still lack drywall and paint. The floors are wet from the rain; there is no glass in the windows. She is alone, all of the men are away. She takes over the camera, records abstract forms and cavities that will soon be a home. A stairway goes to the next floor. We are now on the first floor, in the children's room, next to the hallway, near the stairs that lead up to the attic. Below us is the ground floor. Then we come to the bedroom. From the long hallway, we end up in the bathroom. There's the toilet. A moment later we are in small guest room, still without a floor.

The exponential surge in the production of online videos, and their migration from private to public archives, is a very recent phenomenon. The availability of affordable cameras, bandwidth, production and distribution technologies have made it relatively simple to create, publish and distribute moving images online – generating an immense and ever-increasing collection of personal narratives, self-representative acts, and performances (both conscious and unconscious) resulting from the self-production of media, all made available to anybody with an Internet connection. Depictions of birthday celebrations, fondue parties, the construction of new homes, barbecues and birthdays, feeding babies and holidays, performances, speeches and other testimonials all take place in the private home, yet now they can (and do) have a global audience – of strangers. The willingness of people to publicly broadcast themselves indicates a variety of social phenomena. On one hand, it invites an inquiry into the kinds of documented actions that emerge through self-produced media. On the other, it points to the shifting boundaries between the public and private realms, creating a tension between the public archive and the private experience, between the 'home without boundaries' and the outside world.

> DEPICTIONS OF BIRTHDAY CELEBRATIONS, FONDUE PARTIES, THE CONSTRUCTION OF NEW HOMES, BARBECUES AND BIRTHDAYS, FEEDING BABIES AND HOLIDAYS, PERFORMANCES, SPEECHES AND OTHER TESTIMONIALS ALL TAKE PLACE IN THE PRIVATE HOME, YET NOW THEY CAN (AND DO) HAVE A GLOBAL AUDIENCE – OF STRANGERS.

This tension between the private and the public is magnified even further by the contemporary practice of geo-tagging information. Videos found on the information space of the Web, and associated with a URL, can now also be found in the real world. This happens through the process called geo-tagging, or attaching spatial coordinates to pieces of data, such as a video clips and photographs. Geo-tags can be used to explore a city, in much the same way as search engines are used to explore the virtual, digitised space of the Web. Spatial coordinates can be deliberately added to data by the user; however, people often do not even realise that location information is being added to their files. For example, current-generation Apple 3G iPhones automatically embed highly detailed geo-coordinates whenever an image or video is taken with the camera. At the same time, Public APIs – Application Protocol Interfaces – provided by YouTube, Twitter and Flickr, make it relatively easy to call up, compile and categorise publicly available data generated by these software platforms.

THIS TENSION BETWEEN THE PRIVATE AND THE PUBLIC IS MAGNIFIED EVEN FURTHER BY THE CONTEMPORARY PRACTICE OF GEO-TAGGING INFORMATION.

Several articles and research projects by concerned computer-security experts and hackers have addressed the potential dangers of (deliberately or inadvertently) adding location information to data. Please Rob Me,[2] I Can Stalk U[3] and Creepy[4] are examples of software projects that illustrate how easy it is to collect location-specific digital data and display it on a map – thus providing useful information, such as a person's daily routine, for the would-be stalker or burglar.

In "Cybercasing the Joint: On the Privacy Implications of Geo-Tagging,"[5] Gerald Friedland & Robin Summer attempt to raise critical awareness of emerging privacy threats (for which they have coined the term 'cybercasing') where geo-tagged information can be used to lead to real-world invasions, stalkings, or attacks. In one cybercasing scenario, they attempted to identify the home addresses of people on vacation. Working with a script they wrote using a YouTube API, they searched on the keyword 'kids' in order to locate people's online home videos of their children. Sampling within a radius of 60 miles (approximately 96 km) from downtown Berkeley, California, they were able to find and download 1000 videos of children (the maximum allowed by YouTube). Expanding the radius to 1000 miles (approximately 1600km) increased the number of hits to 50,000 videos. By comparing the two data sets, and identifying only those videos made by matching users, they were able to find 106 videos showing people who were away on vacation. Of these 106, 12 videos seemed to be suitable candidates for cybercasing and potential burglary. One of the videos was uploaded by a man vacationing in the Caribbean, who had posted several other videos from a beach within a period of several days, and otherwise lived with his children in Albany, California.[6]

The scenario of home invasion described by Friedland and Summer, illustrates a recurring theme, in which a contested space, emblematic of the tension between the private and public, is made evident. A stranger comes to someone's home, with nothing but bad intentions. The public, as an external and unknown force, is consequently, or at least potentially, a malevolent entity and a threat to the private domain. Anthony Vidler describes this disturbing moment, when the home which "pretends to afford the utmost security, opens itself up to a secret intrusion of terror."[7] To understand this fear, it is perhaps useful to first provide a historical analysis of its origins. For this, we should look back to the nineteenth century. Scenarios of home invasion make their first appearances in the uncanny stories of E.T.A. Hoffmann.[8] In a recurring theme, a secure and intimate domestic environment is invaded by a threatening foreign presence, turning a familiar setting into an unfamiliar and strange one. Hoffmann's stories, written in the late 19th century, mirror the socio-economic traumas experienced during the rise of industrial capitalism and the subsequent emergence of modern cities, which took place during the eighteenth and nineteenth centuries. The transition to capitalism created an emerging bourgeois class, "the by-products of industrial capitalism,"[9] still insecure about its social identity and position,[10] but also a working class with whom this bourgeois class had an adversarial relationship. The transition to a capitalist system introduced new types of buildings, and brought with it a fundamental change in how public and private lives were lived and perceived.[11]

> THE PUBLIC, AS AN EXTERNAL AND UNKNOWN FORCE, IS CONSEQUENTLY, OR AT LEAST POTENTIALLY, A MALEVOLENT ENTITY AND A THREAT TO THE PRIVATE DOMAIN.

European capitals were physically transformed during the second half of the nineteenth century, re-organised to reflect new bourgeois values: the control of flow, and the visibility of people and public displays, based on the public spectacle of the commodity.[12] The complete redesign of the city of Paris, carried out by Baron Hausmann and Emperor Napoleon III after the revolution of 1848, was characterised by the construction of straight, wide boulevards,[13] with the purpose of promoting the flow of people, traffic and commerce, but also of controlling the working class and asserting the power of the state through monumental architecture meant to "celebrate the values of the new bourgeoisie by prominently housing this class along the boulevards." As Richard Sennett notes, the "right to the city" was defined as something for the bourgeois class, who shopped in department stores, sat in cafés whose windows faced the street, and strolled down Hausmann's expansive boulevards.[14] Public spaces were therefore redesigned to promote a certain type of display and a homogenous mix of people, and to make it very clear that some individuals were not a part of the new 'public.' The commodified world became one of appearances, where interactions in public spaces were not continuous, but based on silent observation. Sennett describes the middle-class 'public' experience of the period, as a state of being amongst a crowd of strangers who are of the same socio-economic class, yet observe each other in silence, without interaction.[15]

THE TRANSITION TO A CAPITALIST SYSTEM INTRODUCED NEW TYPES OF BUILDINGS, AND BROUGHT WITH IT A FUNDAMENTAL CHANGE IN HOW PUBLIC AND PRIVATE LIVES WERE LIVED AND PERCEIVED.

Faced with a complete erosion (or at least a radical shifting) of the parameters of public life, the private middle-class home became increasingly perceived as an idealised refuge, as well as a morally superior space compared to the impersonal and threatening outside world of strangers.[16] The bourgeois home became a protected domain of domestic intimacy where 'real' relationships could take place, turning the potential transgression and invasion of the private home by the outside world into an ever-present source of anxiety and fear. As Sennett concludes, "By contrast, 'private' meant a world where one could express oneself directly as one was touched by another person; private meant a world where interaction reigned, but it must be in secret [...] In the spectacle, few men play an active role." [17]

The social and economic construction of localised identities has been further challenged by the emergence of global economic networks within local geographies. The precariousness of work and of the identity of the worker, generated by the post-indus-trial traumas of the late 20th century, has created a renewed value for physical location, but in a manner that follows the logic of exclusion and intol-erance. [18] This creates new architectures and social structures based on design paradigms of sameness, which discourage and possibly prohibit mixing with strangers. Nan Ellin [19] sees this modern fear played out in home security systems, gated communities and public surveillance, as well as "unending re-ports of danger emitted by the mass-media." Ellin also suggests that "retribalization" and "nostalgia" are modern responses to this fear. Retribalization is a "desire to preserve (or invent) differences," through the forma-tion of distinct groups whose individuals identify with each other and have similar intentions and interests, be they regional, ethnic, cultural or ideological. These forma-tions have been "assisted by transnational culture flows of products, capital, people, and ideas, as well as media." Ellin further elaborates that this retribalization brings with it a sense of nostalgia, a return to the past, to the womb, to the mother, manifested in a renewed interest in architectures that represent the return to 'traditional' values and institutions, such as the return to domesticity and the single-family dwell-ing, a reconstruction of the notion of 'home.' The establishment of a community based on shared interests and desires, combined with a growing 'privatism,' produces homogenised social spaces, in which individuals do not mix with others.

THE BOURGEOIS HOME BECAME A PROTECTED DOMAIN OF DOMESTIC INTIMACY WHERE 'REAL' RELATIONSHIPS COULD TAKE PLACE, TURNING THE POTENTIAL TRANSGRESSION AND INVASION OF THE PRIVATE HOME BY THE OUTSIDE WORLD INTO AN EVER-PRESENT SOURCE OF ANXIETY AND FEAR.

Eli Pariser elaborates on these paradigms of sameness, when he describes how personalisation works to determine what kind of information we become exposed to on the Web. Google, news sources, and social media platforms all utilise algorithms that tailor results according to 'relevance' based on previous user habits, creating 'gated communities' of information by filtering out access to new ideas, people and information. This creates a shift in how information flows online and generates "your own personal unique universe of information that you live online." [20] Faced with digitised information gatekeepers, it is difficult to have any sense of public life, because the possibility of encountering people and phenomena, that do not necessarily fit into what a search engine determines to be one's worldview, is hindered and perhaps even denied.

FACED WITH DIGITISED INFORMATION GATEKEEPERS, IT IS DIFFICULT TO HAVE ANY SENSE OF PUBLIC LIFE, BECAUSE THE POSSIBILITY OF ENCOUNTERING PEOPLE AND PHENOMENA, THAT DO NOT NECESSARILY FIT INTO WHAT A SEARCH ENGINE DETERMINES TO BE ONE'S WORLDVIEW, IS HINDERED AND PERHAPS EVEN DENIED.

Friedland and Summer's cybercasing study, though developed to promote public awareness, has the unintended effect of perpetuating an "architecture of fear" (Nan Ellin), which brings back the nineteenth century threat of home invasion as a twenty-first century unease about the revelatory power of technology, the risk of personal disclosure, and general insecurities about identity, boundaries, and locality. When people are made to fear each other, there is a re-emphasis on the problematic notion of a public space, which is a strange and malevolent threat to the individual and private domain.

Media theorist Geert Lovink, when recently asked to comment on the future of Net politics, challenged both social and informational homogeneity, preferring to actively seek out the foreign and strange: "Let's dream up unlikely relations, spontaneous encounters (and how to solidify them) and technologies that actively derail everyday routines [...] What's missing is the 'sweet stranger' element [...] What's out there are random encounters with a cause. Networks are not just replicates of old ties. They bear the potential of something other, of becoming society. Let's leave the remediation age behind us and start to fool around with dangerous design."[21] Lovink embraces the potential of strangeness within a networked society, by looking at the experience of disorientation upon encountering something that resides outside the comfortable notion of our everyday experience. Spontaneity, randomness and even elements of danger can possibly lead toward something that is unlike the self, and unlike the communities to which this self belongs.

Thinking about Lovink's statement, I cannot help but imagine how this 'dangerous design' might be mapped onto cities. To return to the contemporary practice of geo-tagging media: if online information is increasingly merged with physical geography, produced by people actually living in the city, how could unlikely encounters be experienced in urban space using this media? If media is now connected back onto the city, what are the possibilities for future, alternate ways of exploring urban spaces?

WHEN PEOPLE ARE MADE TO FEAR EACH OTHER, THERE IS A RE-EMPHASIS ON THE PROBLEMATIC NOTION OF A PUBLIC SPACE, WHICH IS A STRANGE AND MALEVOLENT THREAT TO THE INDIVIDUAL AND PRIVATE DOMAIN.

Perhaps mapping information on the web and transposing or layering it back onto the city can lead to unexpected journeys towards places and unexpected encounters with people, in a way that embraces the risk, subversion, playfulness and potential of new experiences resulting from these encounters. This could be described as a type of 'dangerous design-media' acting as a guide towards strangers.

At the risk of leaving all these questions unanswered, and possibly leading to even more questions, I would like to return to a personal experience, that of travelling through a city and trying to find the house that I have watched being built. Having already – virtually – been in the home, I am now travelling towards it. I have a computer on my lap; the satellite imagery and video tell me where to go. After a few dead ends, a wrong turn down a road, a false arrival at a cow pasture, I finally end up at the geo-tagged, recently-constructed family house. The house is now completely finished, the windows fitted with lace-curtains, the façade painted a cheerful yellow. There is no car parked outside, but I hope they will be home. I am deliberately transgressing the ethical, critical, geo-tagged space, by standing at a threshold of the most contested space of conflict between private and public space, at the social and physical border between the private family home and the outside world. Following Friedland and Summer, I have become a cybercaser, but this time my intentions are benevolent. I am standing on the threshold, ready to transgress it.

I am standing on the doorstep. I ring the doorbell.

[1] Clachi70, official YouTube Channel, **"Haus von C&A, es geht zügig voran. Innen tut sich so einiges (Heizung, Sanitar, Wande, Elektro)**, (my translation) July, 2009, http://www.youtube.com/user/clachi70#p/u/30/7v0dd_vwgIA (accessed July 4, 2010)

[2] **Please Rob Me**, http://pleaserobme.com/ (accessed March 15, 2010)

[3] **I Can Stalk U**, http://icanstalku.com/ (accessed March 15, 2010)

[4] Ilektrojohn, **"Creepy: A geolocation information aggregator"**, March, 2010, http://ilektrojohn.github.com/ creepy/ (accessed March 15, 2010)

[5] Official International Computer Science Institute's official Web Site, **"Cybercasing the Joint: On the Privacy Implications of Geotagging"** by Gerald Friedland & Robin Summer, August, 2010, http://www.icsi.berkeley.edu/pubs/ networking/cybercasinghotsec10.pdf (accessed March 20, 2011)

[6] Ibid., 4-5

[7] Anthony Vidler, **The Architectural Uncanny: Essays in the Modern Unhomely** (Cambridge: The MIT Press, 1992), 11

[8] Ibid., 4

[9] Nan Ellin, **"Shelter from the Storm or Form Follows Fear and Vice Versa,"** in **Architecture of Fear,** ed. Nan Ellin (New York: Princeton Architectural Press, 1997), 16

[10] Richard Sennett, **The Fall of Public Man,** (London: Penguin Books, 1974), 130-149

[11] Ellin, op cit, 14-19

[12] David Harvey, **"The Political Economy of Public Space"** in **The Politics of Public Space,** ed Setha Low & Neil Smith (New York: Routledge, 2006), 17-34.

[13] Ellin, op cit., 19

[14] Richard Sennett, **The Fall of Public Man,** (London: Penguin Books, 1974), quoted in David Harvey, **"The Political Economy of Public Space"** in **The Politics of Public Space,** ed. Setha Low & Neil Smith (New York: Routledge, 2006), 17-34

[15] Ibid. 214-217

[16] Ibid. 19-20

[17] Ibid. 17-34

[18] Richard Sennett, **"The Search for a Place in the World"**, in **Architecture of Fear,** ed. Nan Ellin
(New York: Princeton Architectural Press, 1997), 61-62

[19] Ellin, op cit., 25-35

[20] Eli Pariser **"Beware online 'filter bubbles'"**,
March 2011, http://www.ted.com/talks/eli_pariser_beware_online_filter_bubbles.html (accessed March 30, 2011)

[21] Network Politics project Web Site, led by Dr. Joss Hands & Dr. Jussi Parikka, **"Net Activism in the Late 2.0 Era"**, October, 2010, http://www.networkpolitics.org/request-for-comments/geert-lovinks-position-paper
(accessed June 12, 2011)

Benji™: a brief history of the man who brought the intelligence of search engines to our DNA – Amy Suo Wu

"We used to think that our fate was in the stars. Now we know that, in large measure, our fate is in our genes."
– James Dewey Watson

Benji journeys into a world where bio-information is a commodity. It envisions the prospect of more precise genetic discrimination matched with increasingly personalized marketing strategies.

Benji™: a brief history of the man who brought the intelligence of search engines to our DNA – Amy Suo Wu

BENJI™

DNA SEARCH ENGINE

Although Prof. Benji Brin is best known for founding Benji™, the world's leading DNA search engine, he cannot be categorised so simply. If nothing else, his life was too varied, his influence too broad. There are tribesmen in Southern Africa, for example, who know nothing of bioinformatics and Benji™, but know Prof. Benji Brin for his philanthropic work. Likewise, there are factory workers in Albania who know him only as a pioneering scientist; children in China know him as the wise author of their code of destiny; and readers, in dozens of languages, who know him only for his many literary achievements. Prof. Benji Brin is not an easy man to define, and he

certainly does not fit popular misconceptions of him as the aloof and contemplative 'guru scientist'. Yet the more one gets to know this man and his achievements, the more one comes to realise that he was precisely the kind of person who could bring to us the unprecedented DNA search engine, an invention that will continue to shape our world for centuries to come.

Benji Michael Brin was born prematurely, choosing to arrive one week earlier than expected, on December 25th, 2008, in Los Altos Hills, California. The auspicious birth of this remarkable child, on this holiest of days, anticipated a lifetime of faithful reverence, fortune and wisdom. Nestled in his mother's bosom, the new-born infant was serenely calm, yet a certain cheekiness – which would always remain part of his personality – unmistakably glimmered in his eyes. Baby Benji couldn't wait to embrace the world he was destined to change. Naturally, one could say that he was born brazenly defiant of nature's ways, an attitude that brought with it the gift to shape his own fate. And so it seems that from the very beginning, Benji was a self-made person, bound to become the celebrated visionary figure now remembered by billions.

His father, Sergey Brin was the renowned co-founder of the internet giant Google.com, while his biotechnology-savvy mother, Anne Wojcicki, was the co-founder of 23andme.com. In the warm sunshine of their hillside estate grounds, young Benji grew up enchanted by the panoramic view of the valley, as well as the intricate patterns he saw in wondrous life forms no bigger than the tip of his rosy little pinky. At the same time, in the safe confines of his parents' estate, in the comfort of the family library and technological facilities, young Benji already showed a rare talent for computer science. His reading habits were also well beyond his years – philosophy, science and the pillars of Western literature – all part of an effort to satisfy a rare and boundless curiosity. Even before he could fully understand the underlying science, young Benji was keenly aware that his father had inherited from his grandmother a mutation of a gene called LRRK2, which seems to predispose carriers to hereditary Parkinson's disease. As a result, he also spent his formative years pondering the consequences of birth, the fragility of life and the bitter fatality of disease. Eugenia, his grandmother, a Jewish-Russian immigrant and a former computer engineer at NASA, played an important role in young Benji's life. Grandma Gena, as he called her, lovingly nurtured him while his parents were busy with their work, but she also strictly disciplined him when he stepped out of line. She vested in him all the secret knowledge she had acquired during the

> NATURALLY, ONE COULD SAY THAT HE WAS BORN BRAZENLY DEFIANT OF NATURE'S WAYS, AN ATTITUDE THAT BROUGHT WITH IT THE GIFT TO SHAPE HIS OWN FATE.

course of her illustrious career. Stricken with grief, he couldn't bear to think that one day his father and dear grandma Gena would be robbed of their vitality by the mercilessness forces of nature. Young Benji vowed to hunt down and fight what his father euphemistically called 'his personal bug', to demystify once and for all the process of biological breakdown known to humankind as mortality.

In high school, young Benji regularly confounded and stunned his examiners, having previously discussed philosophy with his private tutors, engaged in spirited scientific debate with his parents, and teaching himself the art of meditation. However, there was one specific event, which was to mark the beginning of the first major branch of his career. Obviously, his parents' work brought them into the very nucleus of the American high-tech elite. Their commercial enterprises attracted the best and brightest businessmen, politicians and research scientists, from local Silicon Valley to the farthest corners of the Earth. Celebrities and luminaries such as Natasha Vita-More, Andrew Hessel, Mark Zuckerberg, Severin Schwan, Eugene Kleiner, and the Rockefeller family regularly dropped by for coffee visits or friendly chats. However, one particular person was to radically transform young

> YOUNG BENJI VOWED TO HUNT DOWN AND FIGHT WHAT HIS FATHER EUPHEMISTICALLY CALLED 'HIS PERSONAL BUG', TO DEMYSTIFY ONCE AND FOR ALL THE PROCESS OF BIOLOGICAL BREAKDOWN KNOWN TO HUMANKIND AS MORTALITY.

Benji's view on the mechanisms of life. When he was introduced to Ray Kurzweil, during a dinner party, which his family hosted annually, Benji was absolutely enthralled by Kurzweil's theories of singularity and his admirable quest for transcendence. At last, Benji thought, here was a real chance to provide not only future security for his beloved community, but also to possibility overwrite his family's genetic weakness. Although the encounter left him with many unanswered questions, this was the moment when Benji's enduring passion to harness the mysterious power encrypted in the code of human DNA was born.

With his parents' blessings, Benji was admitted, at the tender age of fifteen, to the prestigious University of Singularity. This in itself was a startling achievement, as he was the youngest applicant ever to join the Exponential Technologies Executive Program, ordinarily reserved for the ranks of venture capitalists, CEOs, strategists, entrepreneurs and government leaders. Already rising above his exceptionally gifted heritage, Benji now showed an extraordinary aptitude for networks and computing systems, biotechnology and bioinformatics. He was a fervent student, excelled in all his classes, and was already close to making his first ground-breaking discovery. As radical as it may have seemed at the time, he had a hunch that the source of all 'original behaviour' takes place at the most fundamental level – the genetic level. He hypothesised that if psychological mood cycles and physical habits could be conquered within the gene, then it should be possible to not only predict and determine, but also to essentially pre-empt, any actual physical manifestations – thus preventing otherwise inevitable diseases, drug addictions and other factors of biological breakdown. It was here that he first began to work out a rudimentary version of his theory of 'DNA Switch Isolation', which he was to further develop in his seminal doctoral thesis. This was the discovery that soon brought Prof. Benji Brin to found Benji™, and ultimately led him to a series of previously unimaginable technological achievements.

> AS RADICAL AS IT MAY HAVE SEEMED AT THE TIME, HE HAD A HUNCH THAT THE SOURCE OF ALL 'ORIGINAL BEHAVIOUR' TAKES PLACE AT THE MOST FUNDAMENTAL LEVEL – THE GENETIC LEVEL.

Among other landmark events, Prof. Benji Brin became the first to scientifically isolate and draw accurate prognostications from DNA, while objectively demonstrating the technological potential of human transcendence well in advance of contemporary scientific thought. His vision of Benji™ was to create the ultimate service: controlling our destiny through DNA. Its goal was to empower individuals while developing new ways of accelerating scientific research and the market-driven economy. Benji™ combined genetics with the ubiquity of the Internet to produce a significant and positive global impact. Using state-of-the-art technology, Benji™ carefully analyses our personal genetic information and matches our data to personalised advertisements, which are guaranteed to enhance our day-to-day life, as well as our long-term health and life expectancy. The company proudly claims that its database contains the most complete health and DNA records of the human race. As the value of genetic information increases, Benji's™ mission has broadened to further improve corporate research of the ways in which genetic data predetermines our lives. In this way Benji™ can continue to provide an increasingly refined and superior service. To assure that the technology is available to all human-kind, Prof. Benji Brin has personally directed the international spread of Benji™, paving the way for the rapidly approaching global enlightenment. Benji™ is a practical service, applicable to every aspect of human existence. It is a service for the here and now. Yet at its core and within each and every Benji™ lies this enduring invitation from its founder: "We are extending to you the precious gift of freedom and immortality – factually, honestly."

THE COMPANY PROUDLY CLAIMS THAT ITS DATABASE CONTAINS THE MOST COMPLETE HEALTH AND DNA RECORDS OF THE HUMAN RACE.

The Spectre
of Anonymity

– Seda Gürses

"Anonymity allows the individual to melt into a body of many, to become a pluralistic one, for which communicating a message is more important than the distinction of the participating individual(s)."

The Spectre of Anonymity

– Seda Gürses

"Anonymity is our first line of defence."
Professor Xavier, X-MEN: First Class

Anonymity is a powerful concept and strategy. It transgresses concepts like authorship, the original, and the origin, and presents itself across important elements of our lives like songs, poems, oral histories, urban legends, conspiracy theories, and chain mails. For centuries, anonymity has been used by communities to articulate their collective voice. This definition is linked to an understanding of anonymity as it relates to individual autonomy, and yet, it shifts the focus from its individual use to its collective effect. Anonymously produced statements or artefacts have expressed the cultural practices, beliefs and norms of the past, while creating a space in which future collectives can manifest themselves.

> ANONYMITY IS ALWAYS A MEANS, NEVER AN END IN ITSELF. HENCE, IT CAN BE UTILISED IN MULTIPLE WAYS FOR A VARIETY OF PURPOSES.

Anonymity allows the individual to melt into a body of many, to become a pluralistic one, for which communicating a message is more important than the distinction of the participating individual(s). Whether at a demonstration or a football match, the power of the anonymous collective produces a field of protection and cohesion around its participating individuals. And yet, the seemingly unbreakable bond can be fragile, since participation is fluid; individuals and groups enter and leave as they please; and, the organisation of the anonymous collective is distributed. The anonymous perseveres only as long as the common line is held. This volatility is also what distinguishes anonymous groups from other collective bodies.

Anonymity is always a means, never an end in itself. Hence, it can be utilised in multiple ways for a variety of purposes. For example, a centrally organised form of anonymity can be found with the uniformed soldiers of a brigade or managers of a corporation -- the latter also known as the "anonymous limited".[1] In organised anonymity, participation is mandatory and actions are heavily controlled. The objective is still to protect, but not necessarily the participating individuals, who are often consumed in the process. Control mechanisms are there to utilise the anonymous group to reify existing power hierarchies, e.g., the state, the nation, or the shareholders, and to render divergences from this goal impossible.

Anonymity, in its more fluid and in its more centrally organised form, when used as a strategy in networked systems like the Internet, operates similarly. As in the physical world, it manifests itself in various mechanisms for a multitude of ends and hence, has different potentials and limitations.

THE POWER OF ANONYMITY IN INTERNET COMMUNICATION HAS LONG BEEN RECOGNISED BY COMPUTER SCIENTISTS AND HACKERS.

The Internet and Anonymity

The power of anonymity in Internet communication has long been recognised by computer scientists and hackers. 'Anonymous communications' technologies -- of which TOR is a popular implementation -- strip messages of any information that could be used to trace them back to their senders, so that individual communication partners are not distinguishable within a set. Observers can see that members of the set are communicating, but cannot distinguish who is communicating with whom, so that individuals in the set are protected against any negative repercussions resulting from disclosure.

Anonymous communications are designed to circumvent the traceability of interactions on the Internet. Its architecture makes it possible to trace all messages, online actions, and other 'data bodies' to their origins, their individual authors in physical space and time; and also to collect, scrutinise, dissect, re-configure, and re-use these data bodies. By masking the origin, anonymous communications channels protect the individuals who author (be it intentionally or unintentionally) these data bodies.

Despite the diversity of the groups and communities using anonymous communications, such technologies are usually cast in a negative light in policy papers and in the media. Anonymous communication infrastructures are generally perceived as providing channels for criminal activity or enabling deviant behaviour. It seems, what bothers authorities the most is not anonymity as such, but rather the characteristics of the user base and the distributed nature of anonymous communications. This becomes evident in the keen interest that data miners and regulators have in a centralised form of anonymity applied to large databases, a strategy that fits squarely with the interests of the growing data economy.

IT SEEMS,
WHAT BOTHERS
AUTHORITIES
THE MOST IS
NOT ANONYMITY
AS SUCH, BUT
RATHER THE
CHARACTERISTICS
OF THE USER
BASE AND THE
DISTRIBUTED NATURE
OF ANONYMOUS
COMMUNICATIONS.

The Market, Governance and Anonymity

We are currently in the midst of an economic hype driven by data. The ideology behind this hype suggests that the data collected is going to make the behaviour of populations more transparent, easier to organise, control, and predict. Data collected en mass is expected to reveal to their collectors ways of improving the efficiency of markets as well as their systems of governance. Improvement comes through mastering the application of statistics to the gathered data sets.

Massively collected, all-encompassing data sets are expected to reveal ways of improving market efficiency and systems of governance, by applying methods of statistical analysis to these data sets and inferring knowledge from these statistics. According to behavioural advertisers and service providers, these data sets are becoming 'placeholders' for understanding populations and allowing organisations to provide them with refined individualised services. In the process, elaborate statistical inferences replace 'subjective' discussions, reflections or processes about societal needs and concerns, as the data has come to speak for itself.

Hence, in this ideology, the promise of control and efficiency lies in data and the processing power of its beholders. However, the collection and processing of such mass amounts of data about consumers or citizens is historically and popularly coupled with a 'privacy problem'. It has been commonly understood that addressing this issue requires limiting the power these organisations can exercise when using this data. These constraints need to hold as long as the people to which the data in a given database relate are uniquely identifiable. It is in this series of reductions of the problem that the data players discover anonymity for their own ends. The database is to be manipulated in such a way that the link between any data body included in the data set and its individual 'author' is concealed, while the usefulness of the data set as a whole is preserved. If this is somehow guaranteed, then the dataset is declared 'anonymised', and it becomes fair game. Inferences can be made freely from the data set as a whole, while ideally no individual participant can be targeted.

> HENCE, IN THIS IDEOLOGY, THE PROMISE OF CONTROL AND EFFICIENCY LIES IN DATA AND THE PROCESSING POWER OF ITS BEHOLDERS.

This approach of massaging data before it becomes mature for release is not only endorsed by data miners, but also reinforced by regulation. The European Data Protection Directive excludes anonymised data sets from its scope[2]. If the database is anonymised, then the data is set free. This free flow of data is then only constrained by the markets, in line with one of the principle objectives of the same Directive.

The Surrogates to Anonymity

What is common to anonymity on the Internet and elsewhere is the breaking of the link between the original author(s) and the message. This is an important element of anonymity as a com-munication strategy. Once the message is released, it is likely to be subverted and reclaimed by others. This is one of the charms of the fluid anonymous message: any individual or group can claim it as their own. But when a group subverts the message to negate all other linkages and continuities, monopolising the in-terpretation of the message's senders, destination, and content, the relationship between 'the anonymous' and the message can become vulnerable.

An example of this kind of dynamic at work, can be seen in Adela Peeva's film "Whose is this song?" [3]. In the documentary, Peeva searches across the Balkans for the origins of an anonymous folk song. In each country or region that she visits the song changes,

"New text was added to that song. Otherwise, we sing it here, too." A dervish from Mac-edonia provides a rare moment of recognizing the ge-nealogy of the folk song.

"The song is Albanian. It is from Korca." The street level expert giving directions to the roots of the song.

BUT WHEN A GROUP SUBVERTS THE MESSAGE TO NEGATE ALL OTHER LINKAGES AND CONTINUITIES, MONOPOLISING THE INTERPRETATION OF THE MESSAGE'S SENDERS, DESTINATION, AND CONTENT, THE RELATIONSHIP BETWEEN 'THE ANONYMOUS' AND THE MESSAGE CAN BECOME VULNERABLE.

becoming a love song, a song of piety, a song about a girl from the village behind the hills, or even a war song. However, with every variation, the question about the song unravels a chorus of claims about its authentic origins. In each claim, the song is cut anew from its traveling past. It is extorted and burdened with carrying the truths of a national past and with shaping the future identity of the referred community in barely subtle archetypes: from the young Turks to amorous Greeks, from proud Albanians to pious Bosnians, from debauch Serbians to superstitious Gypsies, all the way to unwincing Bulgarians.

Peeva's film captures a dilemma that can be associated with any anonymous action or artefact. Anonymity allows for the articulation of a collective message that can travel without the burdens of authorship and origin. However, this void is easily filled when a group, community, or organisation claims and bends the message to suit its own interpretation of the past and future. The message is then fixed, and its interpretation is monopolised. This happens because anonymity frees the message and, hence, inevitably leaves it up for grabs.

If this is the case, the message could even be used to shape the story of the anonymous community that created the message. The anonymous message may boomerang back to hit its

Two steps forward, one step back: on a quest for the origin of a popular folk song, Adela Peeva discovers that the song has also found its place in the repertoire of the Mehter Takimi, the Ottoman Military Marching Band.

"Is this a political thing, or what? This is a provocation!" in response to Adela Peeva playing a religious version of the folk song (kasida) from Bosnia at a Serbian hang out.

authors, often as a collective. The hijacking of popular uprisings by a few that establish their power, the re-writing of folksongs into chauvinistic hymns, the utilisation of anonymous cyber-actions to introduce draconian security measures are examples of such de-contextualised anonymous messages.

In the data economy, the anonymised data set is fashioned as a digital mirror of a populations' activities and tendencies. The organisations that hold a monopoly over these data sets get to assert their own categories of desired and undesired activities as it is seen fit to improve the markets and forms of governance. Since the data in such data sets cannot be directly linked to individuals, privacy is claimed to be intact. Since the data sets are anonymised, the targeted populations cannot expect answers to their questions about the quality, intensity, and use of this data for or against them.

Continuity, Articulation and Anonymity

Given its historical persistence, anonymity appears to be here to stay. It is hence not surprising that this viral strategy replicates itself on the Internet. In its most powerful and at times even heroic moments, it is used to counter targeted surveillance by creating collective protection around individuals. Yet, we also need to recognise that the same strategy is concurrently used to create discrete, de-contextualised, and yet linked data sets, which are imminent to the data economy.

ANONYMITY ALLOWS FOR THE ARTICULATION OF A COLLECTIVE MESSAGE THAT CAN TRAVEL WITHOUT THE BURDENS OF AUTHORSHIP AND ORIGIN.

This economy based on data fetish leads to bizarre collections. We now have gargantuan databases of "friends" who "rate" information to their "like"-ing from which our interests, desires, opinions, and soft spots can be inferred. The anonymisation of these databases is not done to protect the participants of these data sets -- never mind that even in their sophisticated forms these anonymisation techniques provide no formal guarantees[4]. Rather, the strategy is used to disempower their subjects from understanding, scrutinising, and questioning the ways in which these data sets are used to organise and affect their access to resources and connections to a networked world. While we should continue to savour anonymity as a strategy to protect individuals on the Internet, we should reject its reincarnation as an instrument for creating discontinuity between the context in which these data sets were authored and the contexts in which they get used, with the intention to manage and manipulate our lives.

Anonymity will remain a powerful means to achieve political objectives and disseminate collective messages. Hence, the technical instantiation of anonymous communications, must be a fundamental function of our networks. However, especially in political contexts, the vulnerability of the anonymous requires that multiple strategies are available. Different communication channels can be used to create a continuity with activities that are initiated anonymously: these can be political statements that are explicit, precise, courageous, and authored that build on the power of anonymous messages.

[1] A recent article in The Economists states, "In dozens of jurisdictions, from the British Virgin Islands to Delaware, it is possible to register a company while hiding or disguising the ultimate beneficial owner." The Economist, **Corporate Anonymity: Light and Wrong**, Jan 21st 2012: http://www.economist.com/node/21543164 (accessed March 15, 2012) [name of author not given in on-line issue]

[2] European Union (1995). **Data Protection Directive** (Directive 95/46/EC of the European Parliament and of the Council of 24 October 1995 on the protection of individuals with regard to the processing of personal data and on the free movement of such data). http://eur-lex.europa.eu/LexUriServ/LexUriServ. do?uri=CELEX:31995L0046:en:HTML (accessed March 15, 2012)

[3] Adela Peeva, Dir. **Whose Is This Song?**, film, 2003

[4] Arvind Narayanan and Vitaly Shmatikov **"Myths and Fallacies of 'Personally Identifiable Information'"**, Communications of the ACM vol.53, issue. 6, 2010

Dear
Philip E. Agre

– Inge Hoonte

"In a way, it's interesting they've tried to locate you through the very channels you chose to abandon. And now I belong to "them" as well."

March 24, 2011

Dear Philip E. Agre,

Implicit in these letters are some ideas about interpersonal connectivity. Sometimes I poke through the soft, moldable, porous membrane that lies between an attempt to connect, and finding connection. Sometimes I shrub against it without knowing how to penetrate it. Other times I have no desire to come near this dividing line, or I might wait for the other party to make a move. Throughout these movements, a vulnerable web of introspective narratives is woven around the membrane. In deciding to connect, some of these private fragments might be revealed to the public, even if only to one person or a small group of people. This information then has the potential to spread into unknown directions. Parts of your innermost cravings, and unformulated, utter nonsense now belong to other people. You become a story, an example, "this guy I heard about." Other times, you remain hidden.

Mr. Agre, I haven't met you, but you seem to be admired, appreciated, and even loved among colleagues, PhD, graduate, and undergraduate students alike. I'm aware that your former digital newsletter RRE still has over 600 subscribers even though you stopped circulating it seven years ago. I'm also aware that the website, Facebook page, and email group that were set up to update friends, acquaintances, and total strangers of your whereabouts, is filled to the brim with messages from people you may or may not know, urging you to get in touch. In a way, it's interesting they've tried to locate you through the very channels you chose to abandon. And now I belong to "them" as well.

But first I should probably briefly explain my background and intentions for contacting you. I'm a writer, performance, video and sound artist with an interest in how notions of privacy, identity, and behavioral routines shape the tension between reaching out and keeping one's distance in interpersonal communication and interaction. I investigate the space between people, and the attempt to connect with one another across this undetermined terrain: a constantly changing landscape amid physical, emotional, sociopolitical, and psychogeographical boundaries, among many others.

In many of your papers available on your UCLA homepage, you ask readers not to quote from this version, as it probably differs in small ways from the version that appeared in print. I hope you will forgive me for doing so anyway. I've only recently been introduced to your research and writing, and understand that what I'm touching on is just the tip of an iceberg. I'm referring to "an" iceberg and not "the" iceberg, as there are a lot of icebergs out there that I'm unfamiliar with, and I don't exactly know which one, or ones, I'm touching on. In fact, I'm not sure which iceberg you're on, or if you'll ever read this. However, in hopes to carve a way to what lies beneath the ocean's surface, I tried to formulate my thoughts in response to three of your papers in the form of three letters, composed simultaneously. I hope they reach you.

What follows is an attempt to further examine a few fairly independent notes, guided by the scientific, analytic, yet anecdotal style you set out in Writing and Representation (which the beginning of this sentence is also quoted from). The following passage in the introduction of this paper resonated with me in particular: "I often find that philosophy helps to interpret the difficulties that arise in my technical practice. And I want to believe that technical practice can help philosophy. In writing the stories that follow, I have explored some places where technical questions align with philosophical answers. I don't yet know how to convert these answers back into technical practice."

I'd like to come back to this idea of the membrane, which might then also exist, and even be poked through, in the place where philosophical questions could potentially align with technical answers. Within interpersonal communication, there's attempting to connect and finding connection located on either side of the membrane. In addition to investigating the intention of each of these actions, it would be helpful to look at the relationship, tension, and distance between them. But before even beginning to quantify these, one would have to look at the relationship, tension, distance, and commonalities between two other variables that are involved, namely "you," and "me." In my case, it would be fair to say this is a continuation of looking at where this "me" and "you" end, what exists on either side of the membrane, and what happens when little holes are shaped that allow one to move to the other side, however briefly.

This brings me to the first story that I'd like to tell you.

A few days ago, I met a man in a supermarket. On my way to the register, I turned into the coffee and tea isle, and there he was, wearing a sparkly, golden top hat. On a small, white piece of paper attached to his hat with clear tape, it read "3-6-1911." Neatly positioned on the front in squiggly handwriting, it complemented the printed "Congratulations!" My eyes widened, I was halted in my tracks, and after I complemented him on his fabulous hat by muttering only half of the word "wow," we started to talk.

He's turning 100 in a few weeks. He's been interviewed for a program on national TV a few times. When the producer asked what he's going to do on his birthday, he said he wants to spend the night with the Princess. He doesn't need to sleep in the same bed as her, no, he just wants... a kiss. He was unsure if the program will follow up on his wish, and although she has a pretty busy schedule, he was in good hopes that they will. "She's actually in Vietnam right now," and with an endearing smirk on his face, he continued, "Just a kiss..."

While talking, I switched my gaze between his milky, white teeth, and his similarly blurry, blue-grey eyes. I was captivated by their soft, dew-like quality. Locked into these watery, seemingly depthless lookers, I wondered whether all old men have such eyes, weathered by everything they've seen and experienced all these years. There was something about this man. His height and posture, the smirk on his face, the sparkle in his eyes, his obvious zest for things worth celebrating, sharing, and dreaming about in this life... His entire quirky demeanor reminded me of my late grandfather, who I last saw when he was so sick that he slept most of the day.

His frail body tucked in under a thick, grey woolen blanket, my grandfather's eyes scanned the room to look for me every time he came to from a short slumber. I was still there. Glued to the chair next to his bed and reluctant to leave, I held on to each brief moment our eyes met. We both knew this would be the last time we'd see each other, as I had moved abroad recently, and was only visiting for a week. When he passed away a few weeks later, my parents called me in Chicago at four in the morning, so I could be there with them.

But I wasn't. I wasn't physically there. As I couldn't afford a last-minute flight to the Netherlands, I rode my bike out to Lake Michigan to stare out over the water in the direction of my home country to the east. My grandfather's ashes were spread on the same patch of grass as my grandmother's. She died years before him, and he said she regularly visited him those last months. Even now that I've moved back here six years later, I haven't physically been back to any of these places. Traditionally, one could say that he lives on in my memory. To me it often feels as if he's still here, which might be caused by the fact that I haven't not seen him in that room ever since.

That day in the supermarket, I wished the sparkly 99-year old an early happy birthday, and asked what he would do once he reached a century. "I don't know," he said, "I don't know what to expect beyond that."

Best wishes,

Inge Hoonte

April 9, 2011

Dear Phil Agre,

I received an email the other day from a man named Bob Gielow.
In the subject line it read "In Memory of Diane Gielow." I'm not sure
which thoughts came first, but I think it went something like this. In the
same split of a second,

- I was hit by the terrible feeling that someone I knew had
  passed away,
- I recognized the email address as being the joint account of
  Mrs. Gielow, and her husband Bob by the same last name,
- I couldn't remember the woman's first name,
- I was hit by the terrible feeling that someone I knew had
  passed away, and I couldn't remember her first name,
- I knew I met her four years ago in a workshop in New York,
- I remembered being confused when receiving an email from
  Bob Gielow before, which was actually written by the woman
  whose first name I forgot,
- I had a feeling, or I was hoping that her name wasn't Diane,
- I still couldn't remember her first name.

I opened and read the email, and gradually made the connection that it
was not Bob's wife who died, but his mother. Bob, who I've never even
met, but who's probably read a few of the emails I've sent to his wife
Madeline over the years. Madeline, that's her name, not Diane. I wrote
a reply saying my thoughts went out to his loss, but if he could please
take me off the mailinglist as it was a very confusing and alarming
experience to think that Madeline had died, even if only for a split
second. Bob immediately responded, and apologized that I was
included on "this one-time email because I thought my Mom had a
friend named Inge."

What I didn't tell you in my previous letter, Phil, is that I started learning basic computer programming a few months ago. I quickly became interested in the poetic quality of command-line communication, the nature of loops, and dealing with a collection of text as a database of objects that can be manipulated. To establish unexpected connections between data and create new, unexpected narratives and storylines, I wrote a Python script full of loops to link variable Actions (A) to variable Questions (Q) to variable People (P). Inspired by the layout of flowchart models, I then turned to Graphviz, the open source graph visualization software. The program interpreted the textual connections in my script, and enabled me to visualize the connected nodes into a map-like image, such as a PDF format. I've included an image to better illustrate this example.

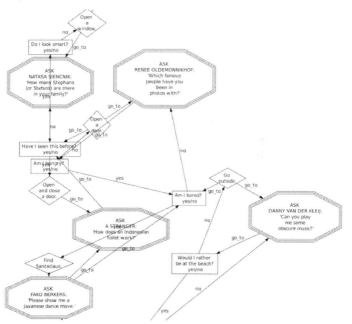

Each group of variables (A, P and Q) was split in half, and then connected to other nodes. There were over 60 nodes involved, in between which over 60 links crisscrossed one another. Thanks to the total amount of variables, and the algorithms that linked them, I was able to generate over 100 different graphic maps. This meant that each copy offered a unique experience of the space the map was portraying, in which the Actions, Questions, and People present shaped the architecture, not the actual physical space.

The script premiered in beta-testing during a performative event. Individual audience members, or players if you will, used the maps to navigate their way through the venue space. Specific questions on the map directed the player to a person who was present on paper as well as in the physical space. As is the risk with beta-testing, there were bugs. In a few renditions of the script, and therefore also in the PDF's, their hard copies, as well as in the live performance of the script, there were dead-end loops causing players to get stuck. If you got to node A5, let's say, it connected to P8, which directed to Q13, and brought you back to A5, through which you ended up at P8 again. As I couldn't rewrite the program to alter the existing printout of the map, the advantage of beta-testing on a live audience allowed me to reroute the player by drawing a new connection between P8 and another node to escape the loop.

However many variables involved, what it comes down to is that the players in this model were subjected to a script. Albeit for the first time, they were mere agents performing a communicative routine through short interactions with strangers. My intention wasn't to create a human metaphor for computation. Ultimately, it became a design tool. I have since read some of your ideas on plan-following, routines, and improvisation within artificial intelligence, and am intrigued by your argumentation for a shift of focus in this field, away from cognition and toward activity. In other words, to no longer confine the digital abstractions through which we have modeled our physical world to the boundaries of the inside of a computer, as if knowledge bound by the dimensions of our own human brain.

But what does this mean? To stop researching "abstract processes in the head," the very way we've always approached mathematic problems, and to look at activity, "concrete undertakings in the world," as you set forth in your article Computation and Human Experience? If I would only look at the actions that are put out by "situated, embodied agents living in the physical world," my own physical world, could I better understand my cognitive motivations for my social behavior?

Your humble correspondent,

Inge Hoonte

June 20, 2011

Dear Phil,

I used to think I'd run into my next boyfriend (a stranger at first) on the Brooklyn side of the Williamsburg Bridge. An avid cyclist with a pretty bike and strong legs, I imagined I would meet him while descending the steep pedestrian and cycle path over the East River in high velocity. One fine day, probably a Friday night between 5 and 7PM, a somewhat distracted, hopeless romantic, equally avid cyclist would come barging around the corner and we'd forcefully slam into each other. Bikes would go flying, we'd be bleeding a little, and WHAM! Love at first sight.

Instead I found myself registered on an online dating site. As you might suspect, getting to know new people in such a way can be awfully daunting. Especially in New York, there's always the chance that someone smarter and better looking is just around the corner, so relationships are short and plenty. Still preferring to bleed for love, I deleted my account after three weeks and two dates.

One day (not on a Friday night), a guy walked up the bottom of the bridge. He was accompanied by a blonde girl, and they managed to take up the entire bike lane that I was quickly approaching them in. Now, this is not the type of descend you can instantly come to a halt on, as the force of slamming your brakes while rapidly going downhill might send you flying. Luckily I was able to avoid crashing into them. Aggravated yet relieved, I realized I'd seen this guy before... The "Jewish Elementary School Teacher," as he nicknamed himself, wore the exact same button-up shirt as in his profile picture on the dating site. But more than his boring shirt, his complete disregard to cyclists was a total turn off. Who does that? Obstructing traffic on the one bridge that's famous among local hospitals for its bicycle accidents. I stopped believing in slamming into true love at the bottom of the bridge right there and then.

When I was subletting an apartment in the south of Rotterdam earlier this year, I commuted to the downtown area every day by bike. To get from south to north, you can either log extra miles and cross the Maas river via the Erasmus Bridge, or you cut underneath the river through the Maastunnel. To get down to the tunnel, you get off your bike and descend a wooden escalator that was installed during World War II. Glancing over at the people who are slowly ascending (and vice versa) is a common daily activity among escalator users. As I have since moved to a neighborhood in the north of Rotterdam, my chances of descending upon true love in slow-motion have massively decreased.

Phil, on many days I find myself preoccupied with what I have recently begun to label as practicing scientific research. My thesis seems to want to answer to the following mathematical theory: the more I reach out to people, the more I desire people to reach out to me. As a mathematical problem, we should be able to define this relationship. To push this one step further, I wonder if I sometimes only send emails in hopes to heighten the cosmic possibility that as soon as I click the refresh button, an anonymous admirer will contact me. As a mathematical problem, we should be able to define this relationship as well. Or as Claude Shannon, the founder of information theory, stated in his famous A Mathematical Theory of Communication: Introduction in 1948: "The choice of a logarithmic base corresponds to the choice of a unit for measuring information."

Approaching the problem from a computational angle, we could compare this behavior to a nested loop within a program. Desire recurs in loops of variable increase and decrease, that respond to an environment with actors that are embodied with emotion, however erratic, lunatic, or random. The time spent in between sending and receiving messages also influences desire. I don't really know how this all relates to age, location, exercise, daily food and alcohol intake, received winks, glances, and other flirtations, the way I feel about my body (hot or not?), the total amount of social interactions in a given time frame, the amount of in-the-zone-type time spent on research, compared to my freelance work load, estrogen levels, melancholy, and many other variables.

This approach is a more positive spin on what you pointed out as a challenge of the always-on world in your article Welcome to the Always-on World, namely addiction. I'm subjected to my own obsessive behavior of mercilessly staying in touch with people, whether I see them once every few years, or every day. As you envisioned in 2001, I now have several portfolios of always-on relationships that accumulate continuously updated information about the people I'm in touch with. Communication devices are smaller, more accessible, and equipped with more communication options. These machines are such a direct extension of my brain and body, that almost every relationship I maintain is a continuous presence that's not only on my mind, but resonates inside my entire body. It's becoming harder and harder to turn off, to be offline, and to be truly alone.

As I've told you in my previous letter, I'm especially interested in the play between hiding and revealing when it comes to desiring to connect to someone. The moment this condition changes, the moment in which what's hidden is revealed, is the moment I'm exposed as having an interest in someone. More crucially, I make the decision, whether intended or not, to point attention to myself by asking for attention, by asking to be acknowledged in someone else's presence. The act through which I'm identified as "attention-seeker" influences the way I perceive and display myself, obsess about how I might come across, what someone might think, as well as how I interpret a possible response. Put this way, it's both a vulnerable and empowering position to be in. Scientifically, it comes down to following the positive outcomes of previous behavior in the pool of experiences, rather than the negative ones.

Thinking about these improvised actions in my interactions with people, I was particularly inspired by the following passage in your paper Computation and Human Experience: "(...) how can activity be both improvised and routine? The answer is that the routine of everyday life is not a matter of performing precisely the same actions every day, as if one were a clockwork device executing a plan. Instead, the routine of everyday life is an emergent phenomenon of moment-to-moment interactions that work out in much the same way from day to day because of the relative stability of our relationships with our environments."

But are our relationships really that stable? Or is it our social behavior that we've formed routines in? And what does a connection even consist of? What are the entry points through which to find companionship? Where do you break through your own routines to find something new? To move away from loneliness and ominous disappointment to surprise yourself? How can I stop bumping into the wall like all the other Lemmings, and inventively penetrate this membrane and actually... fall in love? When I try to connect your view on human activity from the perspective of artificial intelligence, to my own behavior in carrying out hesitant Plans in my dating life, I wonder if it's possible to script quality relationships in everyday life? When considering all agents and environments involved, do you think we could analyze the abstract routines in my dating behavior, and write a script for a successful relationship?

Or are we all just Bees and Penguins, the disembodied agents that act in your Pengi program? Are we doomed to be preoccupied with approaching each other, and running away as soon as danger occurs? Restricted to acting out basic animal survival instincts, the Bee's only way to connect is when stinging the Penguin. The Penguin in turn, can only connect to the Bee by being victimized: stung, killed. Leaving gender aside, does that make me a Bee, or a Penguin? And are these roles really all that different from our everyday lives?

We've come a long way since Claude Shannon deemed the meaning of a message irrelevant, now 60 years ago. With the ever-expanding modern, digital web that distributes and archives our data, I think there's space

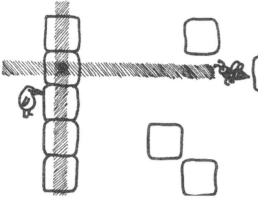

- the-block-I'm-pushing
- the-corridor-I'm-running-along
- the-bee-on-the-other-side-of-this-block-next
- the-block-that-the-block-I-just-kicked-will-(with
- the-bee-that-is-heading-along-the-wall-that the-other-side-of

for "computational models of individual problem-solving," as you wrote in Hierarchy and History in Simon's "Architecture of Complexity," to create islands of meaning in this vast sea of information.

As much as I realized in my first letter that I've only been circling around the tip of an iceberg, I realize at the closing of the third one that this might be as close to the iceberg as I'll get. You might never read this. You might read this and decide not to respond. Or you might find yourself wearing a golden top hat in the coffee isle someday, being approached by a girl like me. Thank you for continuing to work on a vessel upon which to navigate those waters.

Warm wishes,

Inge

Feedback As
Self-performance

— Steve Rushton

"We ourselves are involved in
an information economy every
time we log on to Facebook
or send an e-mail, wherever
the circulation of information
increases our visibility."

Feedback As Capital
Self-performance
– Steve Rushton

The August 28, 2008 issue of Time magazine shows an image of a man who has been caught up in a dispute between drugs gangs in Mexico. He is lying dead in the street, surrounded by a group of onlookers. What makes this a very contemporary image is that the bystanders are taking photos of the man's body with a variety of devices (video, digital, phone cameras). In fact, the people in the picture who are taking a photo of the body almost outnumber those who are not.

> THE ECONOMY OF SUCH AN IMAGE IS FOUNDED ON OUR ACTIVITY AS SELF-PERFORMING SUBJECTS, FEEDING BACK AND EXCHANGING INFORMATION IN ORDER TO IMPROVE OUR STAKE WITHIN THIS ECONOMY.

Making sense of the economy of such an image requires an understanding of a piece of information (in this instance a photograph) as a unit of exchange in which our attention, and the attention of others, is accorded value. We do not know what happened with those pictures of the dead Mexican, but some may have been posted on the Internet to become units of exchange on blogs, on-line communities and chat lines. We ourselves are involved in an information economy every time we log on to Facebook or send an e-mail, wherever the circulation of information increases our visibility. The economy of such an image is founded on our activity as self-performing subjects, feeding back and exchanging information in order to improve our stake within this economy.

This edict to perform has become a foundational part of the structure of contemporary media, in which TV shows stitch together handy-cam footage of hapless viewers bumping into lampposts or falling off ladders, while amateur videos of natural disasters and terrorist attacks provide the 'authentic image' to the aesthetic of print and TV news. Everyday Jocs and Janes confess all, undergo extreme makeovers, have their rides pimped, have their homes refurbished, have their children reconditioned, have their marriages fixed, choose new partners, choose new wallpaper, are fed by celebrity chefs, are starved by personal trainers, run the marathon, make poverty history, bungee-jump wearing a red nose and clown's shoes. In this arena of the information economy, we increasingly use media to police ourselves, maintain ourselves, judge ourselves against others, regulate our behaviour, measure ourselves and measure others. In an era in which direct government intervention is despised (I don't need handouts from Big Government!), new technologies of self-control have grown to replace this intervention, as a greater part of our lives is taken up with the 'work of watching' and the 'work of being watched'.

IN THIS ARENA OF THE INFORMATION ECONOMY, WE INCREASINGLY USE MEDIA TO POLICE OURSELVES, MAINTAIN OURSELVES, JUDGE OURSELVES AGAINST OTHERS, REGULATE OUR BEHAVIOUR, MEASURE OURSELVES AND MEASURE OTHERS.

The reality TV show, for instance, is predicated on the idea of feedback. Indeed, one might understand the new media mix as a circuit of production that collapses the difference between producer and consumer. This has very interesting consequences economically, because although we work in order to make this type of media happen, we are paid little or no money for the work we do – in fact, in most cases we pay out of our own pocket. The profit from our work actually goes to the (TV) production companies, the phone companies and big media conglomerates, along with the media retail outlets that sell us upgraded equipment. As a consequence of all this, we can no longer say we live in 'the society of the spectacle.' We are everything but passive consumers of products; we live in a society of self-performance in which we constantly present ourselves, and excite the interest of others in what we do; and this self-performance is a commodity that has a price. I don't think I'm straying into the realms of science fiction if I suggest that contemporary media have created a form of immediacy in which human subjectivity is the principal object of production and consumption, and in which media serve to facilitate this production and consumption. Laurie Ouellette and James Hay, in Better Living Through Reality TV (2008), link Foucault's idea of 'governmentality' with current liberal strategies of 'privatisation,' 'volunteerism,' 'entrepreneurism,' and 'responsibilisation' which extend media production into the realm of political reasoning. It is the regime of constant testing, perpetual visibility and self-reliance that governs and produces its subject.[1]

So the training and testing which is central to reality TV shows, along with the personal investments in the aims of the show ('this will teach me something, make me a better person'), serve to translate the negatives of travail and ruthless competition into the positives of self-improvement and personal empowerment.

The imperative to perform has been a subject of discussion for some time, of course, and has been variously described as "the experience economy" (Gilmore and Pine), "the immaterial economy" (Lazzarato), "the control society" (Deleuze), "the mode of information" (Poster), "the weightless society" (Leadbeater), "the networked society" (Castells), and as the engine behind "the new spirit of capitalism" (Boltanski & Chiapello). All attempt to explain the shift from a manufacturing society, which is based on physical labour and material products, to a networked society, which is based on the exchange of information. The network, or non-hierarchical 'trading zone' are, as I mentioned before, cybernetic notions, and we use them all the time to understand and 'narrativise' the world we live in. The very idea of feedback within the social network is one of those ideas that shape our world. It is inescapable; but it is possible to trace its origins, chart its effects and establish some sort of critical position.

I DON'T THINK I'M STRAYING INTO THE REALMS OF SCIENCE FICTION IF I SUGGEST THAT CONTEMPORARY MEDIA HAVE CREATED A FORM OF IMMEDIACY IN WHICH HUMAN SUBJECTIVITY IS THE PRINCIPAL OBJECT OF PRODUCTION AND CONSUMPTION, AND IN WHICH MEDIA SERVE TO FACILITATE THIS PRODUCTION AND CONSUMPTION.

For his part, Andrejevic insists on an understanding of capital-ism as a surveillance system that grows more sophisticated as it develops. I find Andrejevic's broad stroke very convincing: since the time of the enclosure of land we have seen a "con-solidation of techniques not only of monitoring workers but of centralising control over the manufacturing process."[2] So the phases are: (a.) the enclosure of land, which peaked in the mid-dle of the eighteenth century; (b.) Taylorism in the nineteenth century (scientific management which resulted in the division of material and mental labour); (c.) Fordism in the twentieth century (subordination of the time of the workers to that of the assembly line and the 'de-naturing' of labour); and (d.) the digital age, which promises to restore time to the individual and release the wage slaves from the factory floor, etc. In fact this promise is not fulfilled, because the digital age actually represents a re-ordering of the relations between production

THE VERY IDEA OF FEEDBACK WITHIN THE SOCIAL NETWORK IS ONE OF THOSE IDEAS THAT SHAPE OUR WORLD.

and consumption, between 'our own time' and 'the company's time.' As we increasingly attempt to sell ourselves as a commodity, our subjecthood becomes one of perpetual presentation; and of course, we seek to find our destiny in the new subjecthood, which we are forced to invent for ourselves.

Andrejevic argues that the panopticism of modernity (sur-veillance through monitoring individuals in the workplace – Taylor's scientific management) has given way, through the processes of new techniques of information management, to the dual action of panopticonism (the few watching the many) and synopticonism (the many watching the few). The synoptic is the regime of the celebrity, of course.

Through the necessary exchange of data about ourselves, we are being herded into what Andrejevic calls a 'digital enclosure' in which our identities (or profiles) can be constructed, in which we can be identified as very particular consumers, and in which ultimately our own performance becomes a commodity for ex-change. So the digital age essentially represents a new discipline of management relations, and perhaps it would be fair to say, a new discipline of self-management – and as the volunteer-

ist models such as The Big Society are rolled out, a new era of
political management.

The feedback loop of reality TV should be understood in this
broader social and technological context, as an agent of governance. The word 'cybernetics' (the science of feedback systems)
shares its etymological roots with the verb 'to govern', incidentally. It is also worth remembering that within cybernetics the
'control' of a system comes from within that system, it is not
imposed from the outside.

How the TV industry understands itself in the light of this shift
to self-performance is demonstrated by Chris
Short, head of interactive media at Endemol
UK, the producers of the reality TV franchise
Big Brother. Back in 2002 he said:

> "We're creating a virtuous circle that
> excites the interactive audience about
> what's going on in the house, drives
> them toward the TV program, the TV
> program will drive them to the inter-
> net, the internet to the other ways they
> can get information, and the other
> ways back to the TV." [3]

AS WE INCREASINGLY
ATTEMPT TO SELL
OURSELVES AS A
COMMODITY, OUR
SUBJECTHOOD
BECOMES ONE
OF PERPETUAL
PRESENTATION;
AND OF COURSE,
WE SEEK TO FIND
OUR DESTINY IN THE
NEW SUBJECTHOOD,
WHICH WE ARE
FORCED TO INVENT
FOR OURSELVES.

The non-scripted TV show is at the high end
of an imperative to perform, which can be seen in any number
of instances where the community is sold back to itself as a
commodity.

To understand how the ontology of television has shifted
during recent years, it is worth looking again at Richard Serra
and Charlotta Schoolman's Television Delivers People (1973),
which came at a time (the early to mid-1970s) when a number of artistic and critical projects suggested alternatives to
the mainstream. These included TVTV (Top Value Television),
Raindance, Videofreek and Ant Farm. Along with them came
a new critical literature, including Michael Shamberg's semi-

nal book Guerrilla Television (1971) and the magazine Radical
Software (1970–1974), which provided a platform for critique
and media activism. All combined the collectivist ideals of the
1960s with the potentially democratising (new) technologies of
video, closed-circuit TV and cable. Here I would like to take a
little time to investigate how these TV Guerrillas helped provide
the conditions that made the current media feedback loop of
self-performance possible.

Back in 1973, the TV audiences described by Serra were 'distracted' by scripted entertainment or information (news and
quiz shows for instance) while advertisers smuggled messages
into their consciousness. The model for the television economy
(in the United States at least) traditionally worked on the principle that the networks would lease programs from production
companies and take in the advertising revenue.

**THE SYNOPTIC IS
THE REGIME OF
THE CELEBRITY, OF
COURSE.** In contrast, Chris Short, our man from
Endemol, describes a media economy in
which the advertiser is no longer necessarily
linked to the show's production, because the
money from telephone calls and SMS text
messages to the show provides at least a portion of its income.
In 2005 Endemol's combined U.S. productions took money
from 300 million calls and SMS messages. Also in 2005, the
U.S. American Idol registered 500 million votes (63 million for
the final) at 99 cents a pop. Although still providing a com-
paratively small portion of the overall budget, these methods
of income generation for programmes are growing fast within
the non-scripted sector of television production, with product
placement – in which products are scripted into non-scripted
shows – rising from a once-negligible share to 10% of the total
share of the income of non-scripted U.S. programmes. Another
source of income which allows production companies to com-
pete (at increasingly tight margins) in an industry where four
out of five new shows fail, is the sale and export of formats in
which the 'playbook' and the 'coach' are provided on a franchise
basis (the European companies Endemol and FreemantleMedia
are very successful at this).[4]

The radical change in the network-advertiser system, which served the industry for decades, is graphically illustrated by the example of the reality TV hit show Survivor. In 2002 CBS agreed to share the advertising revenue from Survivor with its producer, Mark Burnett, who also agreed to pre-sell the sponsorship. Burnett secured eight advertisers who each paid $ 4 million for each show. This was a combination of product placement, commercial time and a link through the website. By contrast, the last season of Friends, which was produced by Warner Brother for NBC, cost $ 7.5 million dollars per episode, with $6 million going to the six principal actors.

Survivor wasn't only cheap to produce (a reality TV show cost $ 700,000 – $ 1,250,000 per hour at the time) and effective at generating advertisement revenue, it was also popular, even outperforming NBC's highly popular and hugely expensive E.R. in ad revenue. The success of the new model represented a tipping point for the broadcasters, and by 2005 20% of primetime programme hours consisted of non-scripted content. This 'Wild West' of television is funded through an increasingly diverse mix of sources, from SMS to product placement and online advertising through web sites that feed into the TV show. Furthermore, increasingly sophisticated techniques for analysing how effective a particular advert might be, have resulted in more diverse and sophisticated targeting strategies by advertisers; a process that will certainly be intensified and refined even further using profiling work from Google and Facebook.[5]

> THE FEEDBACK LOOP OF REALITY TV SHOULD BE UNDERSTOOD IN THIS BROADER SOCIAL AND TECHNOLOGICAL CONTEXT, AS AN AGENT OF GOVERNANCE.

It's ironic that the abolition of the space between production and consumption – which we now see happening as viewers provide funds for production via phone calls to the show, as well as their on-screen and online presence while they deliberate the fate of a particular contestant – was the dream of the architects of the critical, self-initiated media that grew out of the counterculture of the 1960s. They wanted to see the end of the grip, which the networks and advertisers held over the industry.

Central to this critique was the notion that in order to break the circuit of monopoly of production, it was necessary to dive into the feedback loop of self-production. Indeed, the rise of the participant – the self-performing subject – is no coincidence in an economy where visibility itself has become a commodity. In the July 1968 supplement of the Whole Earth Catalog, Ant Farm published their text on the Cowboy Nomad in which they cast themselves as cybernetic cowboy prophets of the future technological revolution:

"YET THERE ARE COWBOY NOMADS TODAY, LIV-ING IN ANOTHER LIFE STYLE AND WAITING FOR ELECTRONIC MEDIA, THAT EVERYONE KNOWS IS DOING IT, TO BLOW THE MINDS OF THE MID-DLE CLASS AMERICAN SUBERBANITE. WHILE THEY WAIT THE COWBOY NO-MADS (OUTLAWS) SMOKE LOCO WEED AROUND ELECTRIC CAMPFILES." [6]

Michael Shamberg, in Guerrilla Televi-sion (1971) wrote about how the feedback technology of TV might be used to break the stronghold the networks and advertis-ers held over the minds of viewers back in the early 1970s: "[strategies] might include tactics like going out to the suburbs with video cameras and taping commuters. The playback could be in people's homes through their normal TV sets. The result might be that business-men would see how wasted they look from buying the subur-ban myth." [7]

> CENTRAL TO THIS CRITIQUE WAS THE NOTION THAT IN ORDER TO BREAK THE CIRCUIT OF MONOPOLY OF PRODUCTION, IT WAS NECESSARY TO DIVE INTO THE FEEDBACK LOOP OF SELF-PRODUCTION.

For both Ant Farm and Shamberg, the subject ready for change is 'the corporation man,' the individuals conditioned by the commodity-centred media to accept their hollow existences and to throw in their lot with the commodity. This is the endpoint of spectacular media: the message (the advert) stops when it hits the consciousness of the consumer, who, intoxicated by the spirit of bad faith, will go forth and buy stuff. Both Ant Farm and Shamberg understood that in order to break the hold of

monopoly, it was necessary to include the viewer into the feedback loop of production: making the viewers visible to themselves would create a shift in the economic logic of the media.
The understanding of TV as a feedback mechanism that could
're-form' an individual's behaviour had already been appreciated by social psychologist Stanley Milgram, who conducted the
infamous "obedience to authority" experiment in 1961. Milgram
was greatly influenced by Allen Funt's Candid Camera (perhaps
the TV format closest to present-day shows).[8] So how do we
explain the schizophrenia of a radicalism that mistrusted (monopoly) technology, and a radicalism that looked to technology
for the solution?

Fred Turner's book From Counterculture
to Cyberculture distinguishes two political trends that emerged in the United States
during the 1960s. These can be broadly
categorised as the 'new left' and the 'counterculture'. The new left emerged from the civil
rights and anti-war movements. This group
understood the world as driven by the material realities of class, race and labour. The
second group, the counterculture, emerged
from a heady blend of beatnik literature and
cybernetics, which understood individuals
and systems (including ecological systems)
as components of networks that exchanged
information with others. In this scheme,

BOTH ANT FARM
AND SHAMBERG
UNDERSTOOD
THAT IN ORDER TO
BREAK THE HOLD
OF MONOPOLY, IT
WAS NECESSARY
TO INCLUDE THE
VIEWER INTO THE
FEEDBACK LOOP
OF PRODUCTION:
MAKING THE
VIEWERS VISIBLE TO
THEMSELVES WOULD
CREATE A SHIFT
IN THE ECONOMIC
LOGIC OF THE MEDIA.

the media could be understood as a media-ecology, the evolu-
tion of which could be redirected. Those experimenting with
LSD understood the drug as a technology of the self, as a form
of software that could change the program of a group or an
individual.
The underlying philosophy of the network was also a major
inspiration for the 700,000 individuals who set up a series of
communities throughout the United States between 1967 and
1971.[9]

By the early 1970s, cybernetic ideas were axiomatic amongst the media activists who had grown through the counterculture of the 1960s; the Portapak and video represented new tools that would extend the scale of human potential, just as every other new technology had done before, while loopholes in licensing regulations (in relation to the new technology of cabal) allowed for new modes of production. As Ant Farm put it, riffing on media theorist Marshall McLuhan's idea of the global village:

HOW LONG WILL IT TAKE THE LAG IN OUTLOOK AND CONSCIOUSNESS TO WHIPLASH FITTING THINKING/IDEAS TO TECHNOLOGICAL CAPABILITIES[10]

THOSE EXPERIMENTING WITH LSD UNDERSTOOD THE DRUG AS A TECHNOLOGY OF THE SELF, AS A FORM OF SOFTWARE THAT COULD CHANGE THE PROGRAM OF A GROUP OR AN INDIVIDUAL.

Shamberg, in Guerrilla Television, made the radical distinction between a materialist left and a cybernetically inclined left: "True cybernetic guerrilla warfare means re-structuring communications, not capturing existing ones"[11] while Timothy Leary, championing the new technology of mind-expanding drugs, stated that "[People should]...drop out, find their own center, turn on, and above all avoid mass movements, mass leadership, mass followers."[12] The imperative for the individual to re-program (rather than for the masses to revolt) reaches its technocratic extreme with Buckminster Fuller's assertion that "revolution by design" will mean that "politics will become obsolete."[13]

During the 1960s and 70s, European media critique (grounded in Marxism) tended to emphasise the alienation engendered by the mass media – the distance between the viewer and the shining world of the commodity. In the United States, by contrast, a network of activists, architects, artists and critics experimented with a different understanding of the medium of TV. Freed from the stranglehold of the networks, accessed by the people, TV could become a technology for 'making' reality. Groups like Ant Farm, Raindance, Radical Software and Videofreek (versed in

the cybernetic lore of Norbert Wiener and Marshall McLuhan)
tested the possibilities of a medium that could indeed produce
a participating network, which would collapse the difference
between performer and producer. What could not be easily fore-
seen though, was how the feedback loop of TV could turn the
commodity and the commodity-performer into same thing. The
feedback loop of non-scripted TV shows is where the contestant and the prize find their equivalence. It is here that the figure
and ground that defined the old mass media are replaced by a
constant oscillation between producer and consumer.

THE IMPERATIVE FOR THE INDIVIDUAL TO RE-PROGRAM (RATHER THAN FOR THE MASSES TO REVOLT) REACHES ITS TECHNOCRATIC EXTREME WITH BUCKMINSTER FULLER'S ASSERTION THAT "REVOLUTION BY DESIGN" WILL MEAN THAT "POLITICS WILL BECOME OBSOLETE."

[1] Laurie Ouellette & James Hay, **Better Living Through Reality TV**, (London: Blackwell Publishing, 2008)

[2] Mark Andrejevic: **Reality TV, The Work of Being Watched** (Maryland: Rowman & Littlefield Publishers, 2004), 23-60

[3] Ted Magder, "**Television 2.0, The Business of American Television in Transition**," in **Reality TV, Remaking Television Culture**, eds. Susan Murry & Laurie Ouellette (New York: New York University Press, 2009), 157

[4] Ibid. 141-152

[5] Ibid. 152-164

[6] Felicity D. Scott, Ant Farm: **Living Archive 7. Allegorical Time Warp: The Media Fallout of July 21, 1969** (New York: Actar, Columbia Gsapp, 2008), 13

[7] David Joselit, **Feedback. Television Against Democracy**, (Massachusetts: MIT Press, 2010), 101

[8] Anna McCarthy, "**Stanley Milgram, Allen Funt and Me**," in Murry & Ouellette, op cit., 23-44

[9] Fred Turner, From **Counterculture to Cyberculture: Stewart Brand, the Whole Earth Network, and the Rise of Digital Utopianism**, (Chicago: University Of Chicago Press 2008), 81

[10] Ibid. 87

[11] Timothy Leary et al., **"The Houseboat Summit Featuring Timothy Leary, Gary Snyder, Alan Watts and Allen Ginsberg"** (1967), (accessed June 2011) http://www.leary.ru/download/leary/T.Leary,%20G.Snyder,%20A.Watts,%20A.Ginsberg%20-%20Summit.pdf (accessed March 16, 2012)

[12] David Joselit **Feedback. Television Against Democracy,** (Massachusetts: MIT Press, 2010), 101

[13] Scott, op cit, 40

A Cosy Place
For Invisible Friends

– Birgit Bachler

"The Facebook 'like' button is a good example of how human affection can be translated into a binary value."

A Cosy Place
For Invisible Friends

– Birgit Bachler

<u>Social networking sites encourage us to believe that our social spaces can be expanded using online services.</u> We presume that communication becomes faster, easier and more efficient. Having a profile on a site like Facebook opens up the endless possibilities of online communication, promises constant connection and offers free sharing with the people in our lives. Facebook claims to be a space for real people, giving them the power to share and make the world a more open and connected place. But how are we handling this power?

> PROVIDING THIS DATA TO FACEBOOK TURNS THE ANONYMOUS WEB USER INTO A PERSON WITH A NAME, AN AGE AND A GENDER.

Before connecting to Facebook, one must fill in a registration form and set up an account. Only registered users can access Facebook, allowing them to find friends, send messages, upload photo albums, write stories and comment on the activities of others.

What social networks are really interested in is their users' personal data, which is of great value to anyone eager to find potential customers (rather than an old high school friend) on Facebook. Personal data is valuable to marketing specialists because it allows them to identify and understand their target groups and target their advertisements directly at potential customers, thereby maximising profit.

The data required to set up a Facebook account includes one's full name, e-mail address, birthday and sex. Providing this data to Facebook turns the anonymous web user into a person with a name, an age and a gender. This data then makes it easier to locate and identify the real-life person behind the profile. Also, the personal data is adapted to fit the requirements of databases. By filling in a registration form, the user agrees to the structure and requirements of text fields and drop-down menus, which helps the network generate a compatible set of data. Jaron Lanier gives this activity the term "personal reductionism," and it is something which has always been present in information systems:

> "You have to declare your status in reductive ways when you file a tax return. Your real life is represented by a silly, phony set of database entries in order for you to make use of a service in an approximate way. Most people are aware of the difference between reality and database entries when they file taxes." [1]

SOCIAL NETWORKING TURNS DIGITAL REDUCTIONISM INTO A CASUAL ELEMENT OF MEDIATING CONTACTS BETWEEN NEW FRIENDS.

Social networking turns digital reductionism into a casual element of mediating contacts between new friends. The Facebook 'like' button is a good example of how human affection can be translated into a binary value. Simply clicking a button supersedes the need to think about writing a personal message. The phrase '1 person likes this' then refers to this one person at least taking note of the content and wishing to make this acknowledgment public to other users. Nothing more, nothing less.

Words such as 'friend' and 'like' are overused terms in the realm of Facebook. They can be deployed to express our appreciation not only of actual people, but also activities, companies, brands and products. Such terms create the feeling of a seemingly personal environment. Everything we 'like' on Facebook becomes part of our profile. We are described through categories such as music, books, games and sports as well as political views and religious beliefs. These descriptions provide the perfect base for categorising our personal preferences into a target group, which is of interest to marketing specialists. While Facebook suggests that creating a profile of ourselves is a way to express who we are to our friends and family, what we are actually doing is filling in a form that makes it easier for algorithms to analyse us.

We even assist in optimising these categorisations of each other's content through participatory surveillance. Because we are visible to people who actually know us, we live under constant mutual scrutiny. The ability to comment and react to each other publicly creates a more clearly defined profile. Our friends will share and tag photos of us, which we would normally not proudly present to the public. This form of participatory surveillance subjects us to the feedback of our circle of friends. We control and govern each other by constantly keeping an eye on our thoughts and actions and the accuracy of our data. In other words, we are faced with (and participate in) something Danah Boyd has described as "invisible audiences."[2] Incidentally, there is no possibility for 'taking back' content once it has been posted online. We are dealing with a new form of publicity within an environment that wrongly suggests that we are surrounded by nothing but friends and likeable things. This is the context in which we must constantly reassess our demands for privacy, as both the rules of the platform and the content are continually changing.

WHILE FACEBOOK SUGGESTS THAT CREATING A PROFILE OF OURSELVES IS A WAY TO EXPRESS WHO WE ARE TO OUR FRIENDS AND FAMILY, WHAT WE ARE ACTUALLY DOING IS FILLING IN A FORM THAT MAKES IT EASIER FOR ALGORITHMS TO ANALYSE US.

"Even though people obviously communicate online with a specific audience in mind, e.g., their friends, the public nature of online social networking makes the information available to a much larger audience, potentially everyone with access to the Internet."[3]

The privacy settings on Facebook allow us to control what we are comfortable with showing and sharing. But we can only choose between a set of options relating to the visibility of content. There is no option for deleting content from the Facebook databases. So being visible is key to having a profile on Facebook. When privacy and visibility are so closely tied together, openness can be mistaken for over-exposure, while reticence may raise suspicion. And perhaps the content that we are not comfortable with publically sharing, says more about who we are and who we want to be, than the content through which we allow ourselves to be defined. We can easily become overwhelmed by the complexity of our social circles, and the multitude of our own identities within those circles, not to mention the possibility of these identities interfering with each other. In the swamp of hundreds of online friends, it's hard to draw a sharp line between public and private content. And as our online networks grow, we run the risk that our engagement with each other becomes less personal and more standardised.

"After our initial introduction to the place and its orgy of transient friendships, most of us only want to bother with people at one degree of separation from ourselves."[4]

WHEN PRIVACY AND VISIBILITY ARE SO CLOSELY TIED TOGETHER, OPENNESS CAN BE MISTAKEN FOR OVER-EXPOSURE, WHILE RETICENCE MAY RAISE SUSPICION.

Managing a multitude of online profiles and contact lists becomes a time-consuming business, whose main benefit is to help maximise the profit of advertisers. So why are we participating in this business of sharing and being shared in order to optimise the profit of others? Mark Andrejevic quotes Toby Lester, who refers to the way consumers are compelled to go online as the "tyranny of convenience."[5] Just as the convenience of shopping online spares us the trouble of going to a store, socialising online spares us the trouble of going out and actually meeting our friends. We should not make the mistake of confusing friendship with a product, which can be easily maintained through a few mouse clicks. And we should be aware that all the time we spend on a social network site, we are feeding the databases with personal, perhaps even intimate data, which is invaluable for Facebook's marketing strategy.

This marketing factor, and the exploitation of the openness of users, will always be the basis of Facebook's success. The promise to only bother users with advertisements they might be interested in, seems to be a winning marketing strategy. Obviously, we accept to generously provide free labour for marketing research, so that we may enjoy the convenience of social network sites. Our online presence becomes a product, interesting for marketers and valuable for Facebook.

As long as we believe that clicking a button can really improve our social status, the trade in our user data will remain big business. While we spend time with our invisible friends online, we risk neglecting our offline relationships. Not only are we responsible for the content we share about ourselves, but also for that which we share about others. In the end we must decide for ourselves, what the role of a commercial website should be when it comes to managing our friendships; and also, how much the limitations of a blue-and-white user interface change the way we see ourselves and our friends.

AND AS OUR ONLINE NETWORKS GROW, WE RUN THE RISK THAT OUR ENGAGEMENT WITH EACH OTHER BECOMES LESS PERSONAL AND MORE STANDARDISED.

[1] Jaron Lanier, **You Are Not A Gadget: A Manifesto,** (New York: Alfred A. Knopf, 2010), 69

[2] Boyd Danah, "**Social Network Sites: Public, Private, or What?**", Knowledge Tree 13, (May 2007)

[3] Anders Albrechtslund, "**Online Social Networking as Participatory Surveillance**", First Monday 13, issue 3-3, (March 2008) http://firstmonday.org/htbin/cgiwrap/bin/ojs/index.php/fm/article/viewArticle/2142/1949 (accessed March 15, 2012)

[4] Harkin James, **Cyburbia** (London: Little, Brown Book Group, 2009), 248

[5] Mark Andrejevic, "**The Work of Being Watched: Interactive Media and the Exploitation of Self-Disclosure,**" Critical Studies in Media Communication 19, Issue 2 (2002), 230 –248

👍 Like

Naked on Pluto: a multiplayer text adventure using Facebook

– Marloes de Valk

"Most people are aware of the existence of the market for personal data; but how it functions — what the further implications are, and what kind of legislation is in place to protect consumers — is unclear to most of us."

Naked on Pluto, a multiplayer text adventure using Facebook

– Marloes de Valk

> "Welcome to Elastic Versailles revision 14. You look fantastic today! Elastic Versailles is here for your convenience, tailored to your needs, offering you the best in entertainment the galaxy has to offer. Win coins in our illustrious casino's, spend coins in our luxurious and exclusive shopping facilities, play games with our friendly bots, socialize with old and new friends, and share your way to a better world!" [1]

Naked on Pluto is a Facebook-based multiplayer text adventure, integrating players' personal data and that of their 'friends' as elements of a satirical and interactive work of fiction. The game calls into question the ways in which social media affect our friendships, and how social relationships have become a commodity for targeted advertising based on the huge quantities of information we voluntarily supply to social media databases – thereby literally exposing ourselves. The game was developed in 2010 as a response to the explosive growth of the market for personal data, and the role of social media in this growth. Inspired on the critical and political text-based games of the eighties, Naked on Pluto combines a playful quest to escape the watchful eye of a corrupted artificial intelligence with serious research on underlying issues of the current crisis in online privacy. This text examines these issues, warns against the illusion of anonymous data, and presents the Naked on Pluto project. We all share a great deal of information with others online.

Not only voluntarily and consciously, through the public side of social media; but also unknowingly, through searching, purchasing and browsing. Furthermore, other areas of the web are endlessly being 'scraped' to complete the (already very detailed) profiles data brokers and profiling companies have on us. Most people are aware of the existence of the market for personal data; but how it functions – what the further implications are, and what kind of legislation is in place to protect consumers – is unclear to most of us.

To some, the trade-off between personal data and free, often customised, services paid for through advertisements seems more than fair. You get as much back as you give. Convenience comes at a price. The problem is that it has become almost impossible to make such trade-offs consciously, with a clear idea of what the consequences will be. Online, it's hard to tell when you're leaving a private space and entering a public one. A great deal of data is harvested without the knowledge of the consumer – not only through scraping and invisible trackers, but also through privacy settings that are intentionally difficult to manage, and set by default to share everything. Furthermore, privacy policies are often incomprehensible to anyone but lawyers. And yet we can't stop sharing. Felix Stalder, in "Autonomy and Control in the Era of Post-Privacy", explains how new forms of sociability have arisen – how, in order to be social in the networked society, we first have to make ourselves visible. In this context, privacy is not a positive right, but in possible threat of disconnection. [2] What is the value of privacy when we rely on visibility in order to socialise?

The 'I've got nothing to hide' argument often proposed in the 'privacy versus security' debate, is not easily countered by a similar one-liner explaining the value of privacy. This is a more complex and abstract story. Whether we're being watched to catch terrorists or to sell products, the aim is always to analyse in order to control. As Bruce Schneier, security technologist and author, points out: "Too many wrongly characterize the debate as 'security versus privacy.' The real choice is liberty versus control. Tyranny, whether it arises under threat of foreign physical attack or under constant domestic authoritative scrutiny, is still tyranny. Liberty requires security without intrusion, security plus privacy. Widespread police surveillance is the very definition of a police state. And that's why we should champion privacy even when we have nothing to hide." [3] Daniel Solove quotes the philosopher John Dewey, explaining how privacy as an individual right furthers the common good. It creates a space for people to breathe, by protecting against excessive intrusion (by states, companies, etc) into our lives. [4] Privacy is social.

The open Web plays an important role in the current crisis in online privacy. Celebrated for its transparency, interoperability and decentralised nature, the Web is not just open and accessible for the benefit of all; it also happens to be extremely suitable for data harvesting, tracking, scraping, data mining, profiling and behavioural advertisement. This tendency is fuelled by (and in turn fuels) a booming industry. On one hand, there is a genuine endeavour towards openness, motivated by a belief in the public good; on the other, there are forces driven by purely commercial goals. How to balance the two?

IT SEEMS, WHAT BOTHERS AUTHORITIES THE MOST IS NOT ANONYMITY AS SUCH, BUT RATHER THE CHARACTERISTICS OF THE USER BASE AND THE DISTRIBUTED NATURE OF ANONYMOUS COMMUNICATIONS.

The free market approach to the protection of privacy assumes self-regulation and consumer responsibility. But when there are no reasonable alternatives for consumers, when a company's privacy policies are unclear, when third parties invisible to the consumer are involved, it becomes impossible to make informed choices; thus governments must define and enforce standards of privacy.

Within the current framework of legislation, too much trust is placed in the mere 'stripping' of data directly identifying a person. With more and more open datasets available, it becomes increasingly easy to de-anonymise data using matching techniques. Peekyou for instance, a 'people search engine', has applied for a patent detailing a method that matches people's real names to the pseudonyms they use on blogs, Twitter and other social networks.[5] A 2006 paper by Narayanan & Shmatikov, researching anonymity in databases, shows how vulnerable 'high-dimensional' data is to de-anonymisation.[6]

Compared to the rapid growth of the market for personal data, legislation to protect users from invasion of privacy is lagging eons behind. Making an 'opt-out' or 'do-not-track' option mandatory (for browsers as well as tracking and profiling companies) would be a good start. But even if the laws were brought up to speed, is it possible to properly enforce them? This would require a close inspection of the code of every single application and online service accessing a user's personal data.

WITHIN THE CURRENT FRAMEWORK OF LEGISLATION, TOO MUCH TRUST IS PLACED IN THE MERE 'STRIPPING' OF DATA DIRECTLY IDENTIFYING A PERSON.

Online games are increasingly popular, while game mechanics are applied extensively in an attempt to generate the same kind of eagerness to participate as experienced during gameplay. Globally, we spend three billion hours per week playing online games.[7] Jane McGonigal suggests using the positive emotions experienced by gamers for the benefit of all. In her talk during TED, in February 2010, she made a strong case for using the 'superpowers' of gamers to solve real-world problems, and to play games that matter.

Using games to address real-world issues is nothing new. For instance, the Landlord's Game, a precursor of the well-known Monopoly, was designed to demonstrate the economic principles of Georgism – in this case, how renting property enriches owners while impoverishing tenants. The idea of the game is to make the economic principles tangible, rather than explaining them. This function of games, generating understanding through experience rather than explanation, is what inspired the Naked on Pluto project to choose an online game as its medium.

The goal of Naked on Pluto is not to directly solve any privacy issues, but simply to make them more tangible. Seeing your own personal information, taken out of context and put in the

hands of strangers, can be upsetting; and the experience of moving about in a world of constant surveillance and scrutiny, is altogether different from reading an article on privacy issues and social media. The game actively engages you and other players in the story, so that you can discover first-hand what's going on behind the façade of this 'brave new world'.

> "I am in the Arrival lobby. There are lines of comfortable black leather benches, a spotless floor, big windows on one side, overlooking the splendid baroque architecture of the Palace, and exits to amusement and shopping facilities. It feels like I've just come home." [8]

The project uses Facebook as its platform for several reasons. First and foremost is scale: Facebook, with five hundred million active users (May 2011) is clearly the most popular social networking service worldwide. [9] Facebook has also done much to fuel discussions about online privacy, with its dubious policy changes and data leaks, as well as the discrepancy between the way it markets itself (open and self-regulatory) and the way it actually functions (a multi-billion-dollar business answering only to its investors). Another appealing aspect of using Facebook as a platform, is that Facebook makes it as easy as possible for anyone, without checking who and why, to access its customers' information. What's known as a 'Facebook application' is not software running on the Facebook platform; it's software running on any server, anywhere, outside of Facebook's control. The 'application' is in fact the authorisation you give to this unknown software to access your data.

Naked on Pluto was inspired by the satirical text-based games popular in the eighties. Two games were particularly thought provoking. The first was Hampstead: the player starts broke and jobless, and attempts to eventually move up to one of London's 'posh' suburbs through a series of professional and lifestyle decisions. The second was Bureaucracy: the player overcomes a series of red-tape obstacles resulting from a recent change of address, eventually exploring the entire universe in order to set things straight. The critical tone and humour of these games were a welcome change from the goblin and wizard-infested text adventures popular at the time, demonstrating that games can be critical as well as entertaining.

> THOSE WHO ALLOW THEMSELVES TO BE IMMERSED IN THIS STRANGE AND DESTABILISING WORLD ARE TREATED TO A SOMEWHAT BIZARRE BUT MAGNIFICENT JOURNEY.

Naked on Pluto's satirical sci-fi atmosphere is created purely through text descriptions. The mix of personal data and fiction, combined with the use of text, appeals directly to players' imaginations. Those who allow themselves to be immersed in this strange and destabilising world are treated to a somewhat bizarre but magnificent journey.

To start playing, you simply log in using your Facebook account. When you enter the game, you find yourself on Pluto, naked as a jaybird, in a city under the rule of Elastic Versailles, a corrupted Artificial Intelligence. After buying yourself some clothes – a cowboy hat, diver's helmet or shepherdess bonnet – you're ready to start exploring the city.

Elastic Versailles appears to the player as a capital of convenience, a non-stop, 24/7 zone of endless pleasure. You can stroll

through the palace gardens, go clubbing, or meet one of the
marketing bots dedicated to making you aware of all the stuff
you want to buy. There isn't a dull moment, with plenty of visi-
tors to talk to, some of whom you might know personally – although it's sometimes hard to tell whether you're dealing with
a friend or a bot. Don't worry if you accidentally find yourself
in a somewhat less polished area of the city: everything is under
control, as long as you return at once to the entertainment
facilities.

Specialised bots such as the 'cleaners' keep the city tidy, putting
all that has been misplaced back where it belongs, giving the
city its elastic appearance. No matter what happens, everything
slowly returns to its original state. Why would anyone possibly
want to change things, when everything has
been so excellently tailored to match your
every desire? But as you progress through
the game, you find out something big has
happened, and as you slowly peel away the
façade, you discover the true nature of Elastic Versailles.

The interface combines two formats: the clas-
sic text-based adventure game (with a prompt
to type in your actions) and the multiple-feed
design of social media. The player is presented with overwhelm-
ing amounts of information, making it a challenge to figure out
what is important and what is not in a 'tweet-like' aggregation
of feeds that is at once familiar and confusing.

> SPECIALISED BOTS SUCH AS THE 'CLEANERS' KEEP THE CITY TIDY, PUTTING ALL THAT HAS BEEN MISPLACED BACK WHERE IT BELONGS, GIVING THE CITY ITS ELASTIC APPEARANCE.

The game requests permission from the user to access and use
non-public profile information. After the start-up screen, users
are prompted to log in to Facebook, after which permission is
once again requested to access certain parts of their Facebook
profile. [10] This requires trust in the application, which is not
easily established. Paradoxically, the more often information
and permission are requested, the less trustworthy the application seems. Even though the game asks for very little information, some users will find it difficult to agree; the 'artistic'

context may give rise to the idea that the game can disturb their Facebook experience, by writing on their 'wall' or changing their profile information – even though this is not possible, since all permissions asked are read-only.

To make sure users understand what the application can and cannot do, the game (free software released under the AGPL license) has a very clear, short and straightforward privacy policy, explaining that the game doesn't store any Facebook information on its servers, other than the player's name and public Facebook ID number. All data generated during the game can be removed on request. All Facebook data used in the game is only displayed to a player locally, on his or her computer – it

cannot be altered by the application, and is not stored on any server, nor shared with any other players.

Even though the developers have provided within the game enough information on any privacy concerns users might have, trust will have to be established, through positive user experiences and word of mouth. The project's makers accept that when dealing with critical users, they will face the same healthy suspicion met by commercial applications. Those who do not grant permission for access to their profile, are likely to already have an informed view of the issues the game is trying to raise.

The development of the game is combined with an investigation into how exposed we are on social networks, how our data is being used, and what this 'second life' in databases means to us. This research is documented on the project's blog, which contains posts on the project's progress, technical development and background. [11] Part of the blog is the Plutonian Striptease series – more than a dozen interviews with experts, owners, users, fans and haters of social media, covering a wide variety of views on this topic. Plutonian Striptease has been continued in the form of a lecture series during the LiWoLi 2011 festival. [12]

> "I am on the Farm. It looks like it was deserted a long time ago. All the windows are broken, the roof has caved in and birds have made nests on top of kitchen cabinets. There are puddles of water on the floor. It smells mouldy." [13]

Naked on Pluto tries to raise awareness of online privacy issues through gameplay and experience, while contextualising the project through its blog. Of course, it will take more than just a game to improve the situation, but together with other endeavours aiming to raise awareness and to tackle through legislation the problems of online privacy, we can only hope that some day the game will become obsolete or unplayable, due to locked-down user data or total refusal by users to agree to grant any third-party applications access to their information. Until that day comes, the game can be played at http://naked-on-pluto.net.

[1] Quote from the game Naked on Pluto, written by Dave Griffiths, Aymeric Mansoux & Marloes de Valk

[2] Felix Stalder, **"Autonomy and Control in the Era of Post-Privacy"**, in Open, issue 19 (2010), 78-86

[3] Bruce Schneier, "The Eternal Value of Privacy", Wired, May 2006, http://www.wired.com/politics/security/commentary/securitymatters/2006/05/70886 (accessed May 20, 2011)

[4] D. J. Solove **"The Meaning and Value of Privacy. Appeal for a Pluralistic Definition of the Concept of Privacy"**, in Open, issue 19 (2010): 34-43

[5] Internet FAQ archives, **"Distributed personal information aggregator"**, January 2010, http://www.faqs.org/patents/app/20100010993 (accessed May 20, 2011)

[6] A. Narayanan & V. Shmatikov, **"How to break anonymity of the netflix prize dataset"**, CoRR abs/cs/0610105 (2006), accessed May 20, 2011, http://arxiv.org/abs/cs/0610105

[7] TED, **"Jane McGonigal: Gaming can make a better world"**, March 2010, http://www.ted.com/talks/jane_mcgonigal_gaming_can_make_a_better_world.html (accessed May 20, 2011)

[8] Quote from the game Naked on Pluto, written by Dave Griffiths, Aymeric Mansoux & Marloes de Valk

[9] Facebook, **"Press room: Statistics"**, May, 2011, http://www.facebook.com/press/info.php?statistics (accessed May 20, 2011)

[10] Naked on Pluto asks for permission to access, read-only, a users basic information, profile information, photos and videos , friends' information and posts in a users' news feed.

[11] The Naked on Pluto blog, **"Naked on Pluto"**, June 2010, http://pluto.kuri.mu (accessed May 20, 2011)

[12] LiWoLi, **"Plutonian Striptease"**, May 2011, http://liwoli.at/programm/2011/plutonian-striptease-introduction (accessed May 20, 2011)

[13] Quote from the game Naked on Pluto, written by Dave Griffiths, Aymeric Mansoux & Marloes de Valk

Network Working Group   Officer 002
Request for Comments: 14   München, Deutschland
                                                October 29 1969

   The Manifestation of Network Anxiety

System Primitives:

   We are the direct manifestation of a Citizen's Network Anxiety; our metal and
   flesh yields from a citizen's networked fears, doubts, delusions and the lies of others.

   We carry the signal and as such are a part of that signal. What passes through
   the air will pass through us.

   We span the space between the invisible and the corporeal; as Adaptors
   comprised of flesh and metal, we capture and reconstruct that which hides in
   the air.

   We are prisms: a citizen's network fears, doubts, delusions, desires and lies will
   be revealed through us.

   We are the lightning in an age of Cloud Computing.

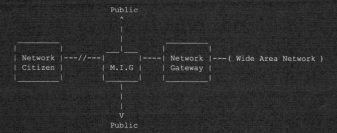

```
                            Public
                              ^
                              |
                              |
    _____       ___|___       _____
   |            |     |       |     |            |
   | Network    |---//---|       |----| Network    |---( Wide Area Network )
   | Citizen    |     | M.I.G |     | Gateway    |
   |_____|     |_____|     |_____|
                              |
                              |
                              |
                              V
                            Public
```

   Figure 1: User accesses distant serving HOST through M.I.G bridge subsystem.
   Packet payloads are reconstructed from network streams and reflected into the
   public.

http://meningrey.net/

sniff scrape crawl

HTML CAPTURE AND
FULL WEB-PAGE RECONSTRUCTION

NETWORK HISTORY PLAYBACK
URL REDIRECTION
DNS SPOOFING

RECONSTRUCTION OF IMAGES
EXTRACTED FROM WIRELESS TRAFFIC

CHAT CAPTURE AND DISPLAY: FACEBOOK, AIM, ICQ, IRC, MSN MESSENGER, YAHOO. TEXT-TO-SPEECH RECITAL OF CHAT.

NETWORK CLIENT HOSTNAME DISCOVERY AND RECITAL

MAN IN THE MIDDLE HIJACK OF NETWORK.

MANIPULATION AND SUBSTITUTION OF: HTML, TEXT, JPEG/GIF/PNG IMAGES

sniff scrape crawl

sniff scrape crawl

Contributors

Birgit Bachler (AT) is a new media artist based in Rotterdam (NL). She holds a BA in Information Design/ Media & Interaction Design and graduated from the Piet Zwart Institute, Master Media Design and Communication: Networked Media, Rotterdam. She has a background in interactive, audiovisual media and programming, and her past research has focused on the influence of emergent media on our everyday lives and how technology influences and manipulates social behavior. By dismantling and manipulating code and mechanisms of seemingly social technologies she creates critical, sometimes playful contemplations of new media. Bachler's recent work features a dating-like website built upon grocery shopping data, an alternative map of Rotterdam based on people's window decorations and a location-based social network of audible content. Bachler has worked with the artist collective Telcosystems since 2008, is involved in the production of Sonic Acts Festival in Amsterdam and member of WORM's medialab moddr_ since 2011.

Seda Gürses (BE) is a researcher working in the group COSIC/ESAT at the Department of Electrical Engineering in K. U. Leuven, Belgium. Her topics of interest include privacy technologies, participatory design, feminist critique of computer science, and online social networks. She has a keen interest in the subject of anonymity in technical as well as cultural contexts, the spectrum being anywhere between anonymous communications and anonymous folk songs. Beyond her academic work, she also collaborates with artistic initiatives including Constant vzw, Bootlab, De-center, ESC in Brussels, Graz and Berlin. You can find more information about her dwellings here:

http://www.esat.kuleuven. be/~sguerses

Inge Hoonte (NL) is a writer, performance, video and sound artist with an interest in how notions of privacy, identity, and behavioural routines shape the tension between reaching out and keeping one's distance in interpersonal communication and physicality. Her writing has been featured by Requited Journal, Curbside Quotidian, Polvo Magazine, Armchair/Shotgun, and the Meeting at the Crossroads Conference.

Inge currently pursuing the Master Media Design and Communication: Networked Media, at the Piet Zwart Institute, Rotterdam (NL). She received her MFA from the School of the Art Institute of Chicago, and has taught at the Academy of Architecture Amsterdam.

Nicolas Malevé (BE) is an artist, software programmer and data activist developing multimedia projects and web applications for and with cultural organizations. His current research work is focused on cartography, information structures, metadata and the means to visually represent them. He lives and works in Barcelona. Since 1998 Nicolas collaborates with Constant, a non-profit association, based and active in Brussels since 1997 in the fields of feminism, copyright alternatives and working through networks.

Works include, Copy.cult and the Original Si(g)n, a project which investigates the alternatives to author's rights and Yoogle! , an online game that allows users to play with the parameters of the Web 2.0 economy and the marketing of personal data.

http://yoogle.be
www.constantvzw.com/copy.cult/
home

Julian Oliver (NZ/DE) is a New Zealander and Critical Engineer based in Berlin. His projects and the occasional paper have been presented at many museums, international electronic-art events and conferences, including the Tate Modern, Transmediale, Ars Electronica, FILE and the Japan Media Arts Festival. Julian's work has received several awards, ranging from technical excellence to artistic invention and interaction design.

Julian has given numerous workshops and master classes in software art, augmented reality, creative hacking, data forensics, computer networking, object-oriented programming for artists, virtual architecture, artistic game-development, information visualisation, UNIX/Linux and open source development practices worldwide. He is a long-time advocate of the use of free software in artistic production, distribution and education.

Steve Rushton (UK/NL) is a founding member of Signal:Noise, an experimental cross-disciplinary research project that aims to explore the influence of cybernetics and information theory on contemporary cultural life by testing out its central idiom, 'feedback', through debates, artworks, publications, performances, events and exhibitions. He has been a writer and editor for a range of projects with artists such as Rod Dickinson and Thomson & Craighead. His publications include the series 'How Media Master Reality' for First/Last Newspaper, Issues 1-6, Dexter Sinister (2009); 'New Walden,' HB2, Issue 1, CAC, Glasgow (2008); Experience, Memory, Re-enactment, Piet Zwart Institute, Rotterdam/Revolver, Frankfurt (with Anke Bangma and Florian Wuest) (2005); The Milgram Re-enactment, Revolver, Frankfurt (2003). He also teaches at the Piet Zwart Institute.

Michelle Teran (CA) is an artist whose practice explores media, performance and the urban environment. Her work critically engages media, connectivity and perception in the city. Her performances and installations repurpose the language of surveillance, cartography and social networks to construct unique scenarios that call conventional power and social relations into question. She is a research fellow within the Norwegian Artistic Research Fellowship Programme at the Bergen Academy of Art and Design, 2010-2013.

Renée Turner (US/NL) is the Director of the Piet Zwart Institute. She also collaborates with Riek Sijbring and Femke Snelting under the name De Geuzen: a foundation for multivisual research. As a collective, their works have been exhibited nationally and internationally at De Appel, Manifesta, the Bienal de Valencia and Stuk. Projects have also been featured in Rhizome, Mute and Thames and Hudson's Internet Art. Parallel to these activities, Turner has produced text-driven pieces for the web that engage in the idiosyncrasies of networked culture. Whether working individually or collaboratively, her projects often employ tactical media to explore female identity, narratives of the archive and online media ecologies. Interdisciplinary education has always been core to her activities. Over the past years, she has taught fine art, design and theory at the Willem de Kooning Academy (NL), St. Joost Art Academy (NL) and the Bergen National Academy of the Arts.

Marloes de Valk (NL) is an artist and writer. As part of the GOTO10, collective from 2005 to 2010, she produced the chmod +x art festival, and co-produced 'make art' 2007 and 2009. Her work consists of, installations and software art. She has exhibited internationally and, led many workshops on Free/Libre/ Open Source Software for artistic, creation. She is editor of the Digital Artists' Handbook (2009) and, the publication FLOSS + Art (Mute Publishing, 2008). The project, Naked on Pluto, was collaboratively developed by Dave Griffiths, Aymeric Mansoux and Marloes de Valk. In 2011, it was awarded the VIDA prize and has been shown across Europe as a part of touring exhibitions such as Robots and Avatars and Funware.

Danja Vasiliev (RU) is working with digital systems, networks and software. His research and practice aimed at re-examination and exploitation of Network paradigms in physical and digital realms. Danja experiments with methods, tactics and techniques that question communication models established between Users and Systems.

Amy Suo Wu (AU/NL) was born in tropical China, raised in the western outskirts of Sydney and currently resides in industrial Rotterdam. Her practice explores the peripheries and overlapping edges where familiarity meets its unfamiliar counterpart. Her research reflects her interests and contemplations on the relationship between science and magic, religion and spirituality, the interplay between history and fiction, and the nullifying contradictions between personal and collective truth. Recent works include making her laptop meditate, flying people to the moon, and predicting the future. She is currently pursuing the Master Media Design and Communication: Networked Media, at the Piet Zwart Institute, Rotterdam (NL).

http://amysuowu.hotglue.me/

Credits

Sniff, Scrape, Crawl…
{on privacy, surveillance
and our shadowy data-
double}

Ed. Renée Turner

A collaboration between
the Piet Zwart Institute
and Creating 010, Rotterdam
University

Executive Director of the
Willem de Kooning Academy
Rotterdam University
Jeroen Chabot

Dean of the Willem de
Kooning Academy Rotterdam
University
Ina J. Klaassen

Director of the Piet Zwart
Institute, Willem de Koon-
ing Academy Rotterdam
University
Renée Turner

Graphic Design:
Gabrielle Marks
Restruct (Timo Klok)

Sniff Scrape Crawl is
typeset with:
Libertinage, Not-Courier
Sans, Junction

Production Coordination:
Vanessa Tuitel

Publisher
Mute, London

Editing of original ISEA
papers:
Joe Monk, Monastic
Languages Services

Subsequent Editing
and Proofing:
Steve Rushton
Renée Turner